P9-BZZ-917

STONEHAM

NOV 2 1 2015

PUBLIC LIBRARY

Pitch
by Pitch

ALSO BY BOB GIBSON
WITH LONNIE WHEELER

Stranger to the Game: The Autobiography of Bob Gibson

Sixty Feet, Six Inches: A Hall of Fame Pitcher &
A Hall of Fame Hitter Talk About How the Game Is Played
by Bob Gibson and Reggie Jackson with Lonnie Wheeler

Pitch by Pitch

*My View of
One Unforgettable Game*

BOB GIBSON
WITH LONNIE WHEELER

FLATIRON
BOOKS
NEW YORK

PITCH BY PITCH. Copyright © 2015 by Bob Gibson and Lonnie Wheeler.
All rights reserved. Printed in the United States of America. For information,
address Flatiron Books, 175 Fifth Avenue, New York, N.Y. 10010.

www.flatironbooks.com

The Library of Congress Cataloging-in-Publication Data is available upon request.

ISBN 978-1-250-06104-1 (hardcover)
ISBN 978-1-250-06069-3 (e-book)

Our books may be purchased in bulk for promotional, educational, or
business use. Please contact your local bookseller or the Macmillan
Corporate and Premium Sales Department at (800) 221-7945, extension
5442, or by e-mail at MacmillanSpecialMarkets@macmillan.com.

First Edition: October 2015

10 9 8 7 6 5 4 3 2 1

Contents

Pitch
by Pitch

(NEIL LEIFER/GETTY IMAGES)

These were the guys who would take on the Detroit Tigers in game one of the 1968 World Series. They were the very same fellows who had successfully opposed the Boston Red Sox a year before, batting in the very same order. First row, from left: Mike Shannon (third base, batting sixth), Dal Maxvill (shortstop, batting eighth), and Lou Brock (left field, leading off). Second row: manager Red Schoendienst, me (pitching and batting ninth), my pal Curt Flood (center field, batting second), and Julian Javier (second base, batting seventh). Third row: Orlando Cepeda (first base, cleanup). Fourth row: my battery mate, Tim McCarver (catcher, batting fifth). In the back, making himself comfortable: Roger Maris (right field, batting third).

Pregame

THERE IS MUCH I don't remember about the afternoon of October second, a muggy Wednesday in the Year of the Pitcher. It was, after all, forty-seven autumns ago, although, I have to say, I wouldn't have recalled a whole lot about that day even if you'd asked about it that night. October second was my thirty-fifth pitching day of 1968, and on pitching days—especially those in the World Series—I wouldn't have noticed a barking elephant if it wore a flowered hat and sat in the commissioner's popcorn. Whatever happened, if it didn't happen in Tim Mc-Carver's mitt, I probably missed it.

So I have no recollection of the events that accompanied or preceded those nine innings, such as, say, what I ate for breakfast that morning, except that, in the case of breakfast, I can testify that it probably wasn't pancakes and sausage because food didn't particularly interest me on pitching days. The year before, on the morning of game seven in Boston, I'd had scrambled eggs in mind, in part because the air-conditioning at our hotel didn't work and I hadn't slept too well, but after forty-five minutes of waiting for my order in the restaurant off the lobby, during which time my wife and the McCarvers and Dal Maxvill and his wife had all been served, the waitress brought me some blackened toast, which led to a lively discussion between the two of us. When my displeasure had been satisfactorily vented, I marched my empty stomach straight to the bus, which had been delayed on my behalf, and ultimately did just fine on a ham-and-egg sandwich that Bob Broeg of the *St. Louis Post-Dispatch* picked up for me at a diner and brought to the clubhouse. Actually, he brought me two of them, but I stashed the other one in my locker for after the game, which we won on a three-hitter. I could pitch hungry.

Even the pregame machinations of the Cardinal clubhouse were mostly beyond the pale of my cognizance, it being my custom to catch a few winks about an hour before taking the mound. After batting practice I'd get comfortable on the training table and when Doc Bauman was finished massaging and stretching my arm he'd pull a towel over my head to muffle my snoring.

I tended not to talk to people on the days I pitched, and people tended not to talk to me, but the World Series attracts fair-weather media types who aren't up to speed on the protocol. In the early afternoon of October second, one of them, a television reporter, asked me, unadvisedly, what I thought of the civil rights rally held that morning under the Gateway Arch, which was only a few blocks away, towering over the left-field scoreboard of Busch Memorial Stadium. Ordinarily, and particularly in 1968, I was sensitive to those kinds of things, and willing to share the awesome wisdom of my opinions—but not on pitching days, for pity's sake. Certainly not on *this* pitching day. My mind was where it needed to be, and the very thing I wanted least, just before my biggest start of the season, was a distraction. I told the guy I didn't give a hoot, only I didn't say hoot (which happens to be a nickname of mine). Instead, I used a word of the same length that ensured my answer wouldn't grace the broadcast. Anyway, I had already offered my statement on racial questions with a button I placed over my locker before the Series. It said, "I'm not prejudiced. I hate everybody."

But we were talking about things that escaped my attention on every fifth day of the baseball season. Needless to say, I knew nothing, on October second, of the Tlatelolco Massacre—1968, you may recall, was the year of much more than the pitcher, in many more countries than our own—in which hordes of protesting students were killed that day and night by police and military personnel in Mexico City.

I do, however, have a vivid memory of high fastballs to Norm Cash and tight sliders on the hands of Willie Horton. And for the less indelible pitches, there's a video.

On the video, which is black and white and blurry, I enter the scene in full stride, booking toward my workstation, appearing ready and eager but rather puzzled. As I approach the base of the mound I squint toward home plate, then the other way, then back again, as if searching for an usher, an explanation, a rest room, something. The first time or two I watched, I wondered what in the hell I was hoping to see out there. Finally, after one more rewind, I took note of the younger me reaching out with the glove, and I realized: of course, I was looking for *the ball*. I was thinking, *Come on, who's got the damn ball? Let's go!*

BY THE FIRST of September, when we led the National League by thirteen games, we knew damn well we'd be playing in the World Series. Within a couple weeks, the Detroit Tigers, ahead by ten and a half in the American League, had removed any lingering uncertainty in the question of our opponent. No team would ever again find itself in the position we enjoyed in late '68.

The playoffs, which began in 1969, added a round of suspense and good baseball—then two rounds, now two and a quickie qualifier—to the postseason; but there was a price to pay in purity. No longer does the World Series come with a guarantee that it will match the American League's best team against the National's, as determined by victories earned over six demanding months of championship competition.

For the Cardinals, the upshot was that we had a month to prepare for one team and seven games. Of course, in my case that didn't make much difference. While it gave us an extended look at the Tigers, the Tigers were able to train their sights on us all the while; and I didn't put a lot of stock in scouting reports, anyway, for reasons I'll get into later.

Nor did I bother to pace myself in September. Staying on schedule, I started six games that month and pitched every inning of them but one, which was the only regulation inning I'd missed since late May (I did sit out the twelfth and thirteenth on a Sunday in early August). The first of those outings was a ten-inning 1–0 win at Cincinnati. The last, my 22nd victory, was a 1–0 decision over the Astros at Busch Stadium, and it left me with my regular four days of rest for the opener of the World Series. Perfect. I had a rhythm working and didn't care to trifle with it.

The final shutout—it was my thirteenth, which led both leagues and more than doubled my total from any other season—brought my earned run average down from 1.16 to 1.12, which is considered the record in the modern era. Some people assumed that the ERA record was my incentive for pitching nine innings that night, on the brink of the Series, in a game that had no pennant implications. I can assure you, that was not a factor. I didn't even know about it until after the game. Wasn't interested in that kind of thing. There was only one statistic that might have—no, *would have*—motivated me in that respect: 20 wins. In fact, it happened that way in 1965, when I won my 20th game on the final day of the season. The same scenario would come up again in 1969, and that time I had to go twelve innings to get number 20. I would have pitched *another* twelve if I had to. These days, sabermetricians tell us that wins are a poor way to judge a starting pitcher. To me, they were everything.

Consequently, I had a good bit of admiration, and maybe a touch of envy, for the Tigers' ace, Denny McLain. While Detroit was running away with the '68 pennant, McLain, at the age of twenty-four, was becoming the first pitcher to win 30 games since the colorful old Cardinal, Dizzy Dean, in 1934, which happened to be the last time the Cardinals and Tigers had met in the World Series. In fact, McLain, with an outstanding 1.96 ERA, won 31. He was on *The Ed Sullivan Show* and the cover of *Time*. But that's not what made me jealous.

The thing he had that I coveted—along with the nine more victories—was run support. The Tigers scored at least four runs for McLain on twenty-nine occasions that year. By contrast, the Cardinals—and please don't get me wrong, I loved my ball club—scored as many as four runs in only a dozen of the games I pitched. McLain received at least three runs in thirty-four of his forty-one starts. The Cardinals scored three runs or more in sixteen of mine. To be fair, McLain, who often worked with only three days of rest, took the ball seven more times than I did. The '68 season marked the first time I'd thrown 300 innings—a fraction over 304—but McLain put up 336 with a sore shoulder and regular cortisone shots. He was cocky, controversial, and, indisputably, a stud.

He was also my opponent in game one of the World Series, which, naturally, was a cherry-pick story line for the national media. I had nothing to add on that subject. McLain, however, did. "I'm sick of hearing what a great team the Cardinals are," he said. "I don't want to just beat them; I want to demolish them."

I'd have been more interested in McLain's remarks—as I'd been with Carl Yastrzemski's in 1967, when he predicted our demise and licked his chops at the thought of facing me—if he batted in the middle of the Tigers' order. As it was, I didn't have to give him much thought. I was infinitely more concerned with Horton and Cash and a loaded Detroit lineup that had led the American League in runs and all of baseball in homers. By a lot.

(Copyright Bettmann/Corbis/AP Images)

The first pitch of the game was a fastball, high and outside, to Dick McAuliffe, the Tigers' scrappy second baseman. By this point, McAuliffe had lowered his bat from the peculiar position—ear level, ahead of his face—in which he held it when he assumed his radically open, highly unusual stance.

First Inning

IN 1968, I hated the first inning a little less than I had before. Over my career, the first, for me, was the worst of times. My earned run average for the first inning was an even 4.00, more than a run higher than the rest of the game. In the second, it plummeted to about half that much.

The problem, mainly, was control. Over my seventeen years in the big leagues, I walked 203 batters in the first inning, which was 37 more than any other. That might not sound so terrible, but consider that the leadoff and second hitters are typically Punch-and-Judy guys who have not earned the privilege of being pitched to carefully. I was loath to put a batter like that on base without giving him a chance to send Curt Flood a lovely can of corn. I'd pour it at him and let the little fellow hack away to his heart's content. At least, that was my intention. And yet, time and again, year after year, I began the game by letting one of those nuisances off the hook with four infuriating balls. Walking a singles hitter was a sin, and I was a wretched first-inning reprobate. To make it worse, the leadoff spot piled up a better batting average against me than any other place in the lineup, followed by the two hole, followed by the three. Inning one was my Valley of Doom.

For a long time, I assumed that I was warming up improperly in the bullpen. So I fooled around with different routines. I tried throwing for seven or eight minutes, sitting down for a while, then throwing another for seven or eight, simulating the flow of the game. Didn't help. Other times I'd crank up the velocity and effort level. Nothing seemed to make a difference. One night, I thought I'd stumbled upon a miracle cure. I'd washed my car that afternoon, then went out and pitched a gem with some of my best stuff of the season. Voilà! Naturally, I was out there soaping and scrubbing again five days later. Got lit up that night. There was another time when I shut somebody down after having an argument earlier in the day with my wife; but I didn't think it advisable to make a habit out of that. So I just stayed the course with what seemed sensible: loosening up, getting a feel for the breaking ball, finding the corners, and going all-out for the last few pitches.

Then, in 1968, the problem was suddenly solved. The breakthrough wasn't in my warm-up; it was in my control.

My ability to put the ball where I wanted it had been improving, if sometimes negligibly, since midway through the summer of 1961, when Johnny Keane relieved Solly Hemus as the Cardinal manager. I'd been unpolished when I arrived in St. Louis in 1959, and that might be an understatement—I led the league in walks in '61, my first year in the rotation—but my pitching skills weren't as hopeless as Hemus would have had me think. He held them in such contempt that, when he went over an opposing team's scouting report with the pitching staff, he'd pause and tell me not to worry about all that stuff, just try to throw some strikes. Maybe that's why I felt as I did about scouting reports. And Solly Hemus.

Johnny Keane, on the other hand, a milder man who had studied for the priesthood, was a cultivator and guardian of my confidence, which is something a pitcher requires when he's trying to locate a hard slider on the edge of the plate under the glare of thirty thousand people, including a couple base runners and, sixty and a half feet away, Hank Aaron. Or any other time he lets it fly. Although Keane was long gone by 1968, supplanted by Red Schoendienst, I truly believe that my success that year was mostly attributable to the trust I had that the ball was going to end up right where it was supposed to. To a degree that impressed both me and McCarver, it did so with inspiring regularity. I had become a control pitcher. Fastball, breaking ball; didn't matter. In 1968, I felt that I could close my eyes and sling the thing behind my back—I'd been a Harlem Globetrotter, after all—and it would find its way to the outside corner. The baseball had become my smart bomb.

Nevertheless, my first pitch to Dick McAuliffe was considerably high and outside. McCarver put his target in the center of the plate, at the top of McAuliffe's thigh, and I made him stand up, reaching left, to catch it.

I SUPPOSE YOU could blame that one on the World Series.

You'd think, by then, I wouldn't have let it get to me. I'd started three Series games in 1964 when we beat the Yankees and three more in 1967 when we beat the Red Sox, won the last five of them, which left me tied for the National League record, and been named the Series MVP on both occasions. So I wasn't awed and I wasn't frightened and I wasn't trying to do more than I'd done before. The only thing new to my experience was pitching game one in front of the home crowd, which happened to be the largest crowd in the history of Busch Stadium, with everybody a little louder than usual, and dressed better, in spite of so many men wearing silly white straw hats, courtesy of some giveaway or another. Like any World Series, there were cameras and umpires everywhere. None of that rattled me. But my adrenaline ran on pride, and my pride was fed by winning, and the World Series made my stomach growl. I was overeager, is all. A little *too* hungry. It only lasted a pitch.

The second one was another fastball, a four-seamer about 96 or 97 miles an hour on the inside corner at the waist, cutting toward McAuliffe's hands. Because of the action on it, a lot of batters mistook my four-seam fastball for a slider. I didn't change my grip to cut the ball that way—and we didn't call it a *cutter* in those days—but I held the four-seamer on the side a little bit and the movement happened naturally. McCarver says it was because of my deformed fingers. I wouldn't describe them that way, but my fingers are oddly symmetrical. My little finger matches my index finger in length, and the middle two stand even, as well. I have no idea what effect that might have had on the geometry of my pitches, but I do know that it had less—if there was any to start with—when I threw the four-seamer down in the strike zone, which I didn't do often. The four-seamer was the faster of my two fastballs, and I preferred to elevate it, especially to left-handers, like McAuliffe, who had to turn things up a notch to handle a pitch boring in on their fists at that speed. It was important to find out, as soon as possible, if he could do that. McAuliffe was a batter with whom I took nothing at face value.

I paid attention to a batter's stance, and generally factored it into my approach, but it can be hazardous to draw hard conclusions from such superficial information. For one thing, nearly every batter arrives at the same position to address the ball. For another, there was Dick McAuliffe. The Tigers' second baseman stood with his back foot close to the plate, his shoulders and hips pointed to first base, and his bat held up at ear level, his hands actually out in front of his nose. When a guy sets up with a dramatically open stance like that, it's tempting to assume he can't reach a pitch on the outside half of the plate. On the other hand, he has to close his stance and stride forward as he approaches the ball, which, ordinarily, made me inclined to bust him inside. But McAuliffe added a twist to that norm. After he picked up his right foot to start his swing and, ostensibly, square his body, he would put it down very close to where it had been to begin with. His shoulders never really squared. Even as the first pitch sailed outside, his motion had kept him positioned to pull it, if he could.

McAuliffe was unconventional in more ways than just that. He didn't fit the profile of a leadoff hitter. While he had the size and scrappiness associated with that spot, he didn't bat for a high average. He did, however, collect a fair number of home runs—16 that year, after three of the previous four seasons in the low 20s. I respected power. I also respected McAuliffe's competitiveness. In August, he'd earned a five-game suspension for rushing the mound and separating Tommy John's shoulder after John had buzzed him twice. His teammates called him Mad Dog. They knew better than to try to engage him in conversation before a ball game. He was the kind of player I could appreciate.

He was also one who thrived on challenges, much like me. Challenging, in pitching parlance, involves fastballs on the inner half of the plate, a standard point of origin for long flies that reach the seats. There was significant risk in challenging a guy with McAuliffe's home run potential; but I wasn't inclined to tread lightly with the leadoff hitter. The Tigers had enough big boppers in the middle of the order for whom I'd have to reserve my discretion. McAuliffe was getting the fastball in. I don't recall what the scouting report suggested for him, because I didn't pay it a lot of attention—the reports were based on what the Detroit hitters did against the fastballs and sliders of *other* pitchers, not mine—but I'm pretty sure it wasn't that. I didn't care. I needed to get started with my *own* scouting. McAuliffe, matching no familiar stereotype, was the kind of hitter I'd have to figure out for myself, probing, mixing, and challenging.

He swung from his heels and missed.

I went next with a slider away. It was the pitch that McCarver believed, and still believes—I don't disagree with him, which is a little unusual, in spite of our fast friendship—carried me to a higher level in 1968. In spring training that year, Tim had encouraged me to throw it. I'd always had difficulty controlling my breaking pitches on the arm side of the plate, which is outside to a left-handed hitter, and was reluctant to throw a slider that I was afraid might sweep right into the sweet spot over the middle. But McCarver convinced me that my control had improved enough that I could now deliver that pitch with conviction. He was right, and it made a profound difference. Left-handers were still the hitters that most threatened me, as a rule, but in 1968 I felt that I'd finally grabbed the upper hand against them. The numbers bore that out.

This slider, however, sailed high and wide for ball two.

McAuliffe hadn't yet seen the two-seam fastball. Because of the spin that carries it downward, the two-seamer is a heavier pitch than the four-seam fastball. With the sinking action, though, I wouldn't throw it inside to a left-handed hitter. For the most part, I didn't like to deliver *anything* down and in to lefties, because a pitch there is too easy for them to reach and rip by turning—McAuliffe, of course, was *already* turned—and dropping the bat head. I wouldn't have minded putting the two-seamer in that spot if I'd been able to start it off the inside corner to a left-hander and make it curl back for a strike, the pitch that Greg Maddux later perfected. But since I couldn't pull that off, I tried to keep it on the outer edge. The two-seamer to McAuliffe didn't quite make it there. It was down and centered, but that was effectively outside to him. He popped it foul on the third-base side, behind the Tigers' dugout, out of Mike Shannon's reach.

With the two-seamer on a 2-1 count, my preference would have been a ground ball to Julian Javier at second base. But now I was in strikeout position. Of the four pitches I'd thrown to McAuliffe, only one had resulted in a swing and miss. I went with another four-seamer at the belt, and got the same result.

NOT LONG AGO I was sitting in a St. Louis restaurant, near the new Busch Stadium, with Tim McCarver, and we were talking about my curveball. Actually, *I* was talking about my curveball, and he was swearing I never threw one. This is the man who caught me for seven full years and parts of three others. The man with whom, on the ball field, I shared such a singleness of mind that I'd often start my motion before he was finished giving his sign. The man with whom, off the field, I treasured a connection that, from the time we met in 1959—me a blunt, stubborn black man and Tim a rugged white teenager from Memphis,

Tennessee, with all the sensibilities which that implies—had evolved both unforeseeably and wonderfully.

When Tim called for a slider, I was liable to throw him either of two breaking pitches. The main one, released with a stiff wrist, was a hard slider with good velocity—I'd estimate that, at least early in my career, it would reach as high as about 92 miles an hour—and a tight, darting downturn. But less often, I'd roll my wrist and the ball would come in slower and loopier, with a much bigger break. Tim always thought the off-speed, bigger-breaking ball was just a variation on the slider. To me, it was a curveball. That night over dinner, I finally got around to explaining this. McCarver was incredulous.

"How was I supposed to figure out what's coming?"

"I never realized you didn't know," I told him.

He paused for a moment, then held up the meaty palm that he had crammed inside his catcher's mitt for twenty big-league seasons. "I've been having trouble with my left hand," he said. "And I know for a fact that the reason I'm having this problem is the same reason the hitters did when they faced you. They couldn't predict where the ball was going, and neither could I. Nothing wore me out like you did. After the sixth or seventh inning, my third or fourth at-bat, I'd be hitting with eight fingers. The burning of the bone. The result is, I think of you every day of my life."

"You knew it was a breaking ball. I figured, you're a catcher—catch it. That was the mentality. I didn't realize how difficult it was. You always caught it."

"It's okay," he said quietly. "It's all made up for by what you accomplished."

"If I had to do it over again, Tim, I'd tell you what was coming."

It was a curveball that I threw on the first pitch to the Tigers' second batter, Mickey Stanley, who fouled it back to the right side, his body pulling out as he reached across the plate with his bat. If it had been a slider, he wouldn't have been so far out in front of it.

Stanley, a right-handed hitter, had been Detroit's starting center fielder all season, and some considered him the best in the American League at that position. Willie Horton, the Tigers' most dangerous power threat, manned left field, and when Al Kaline, their future Hall of Famer, broke his arm in May, Jim Northrup took over in right, eventually leading the club in RBIs. Kaline played a part-time role after he returned, but he'd gotten stronger late in the season and the Tigers' manager, Mayo Smith, was determined to find a starting spot for him in Kaline's first World Series, at the age of thirty-three. The solution—reportedly at the urging of Norm Cash—was to restore Kaline to right field, shuffle Northrup to center, and bring Stanley in to play short-stop. He'd never played short before, and it's probably the most demanding position outside of catcher (and pitcher, of course), but Stanley was considered the Tigers' best all-around athlete and was gifted with the glove. As a trial run, Smith started him at shortstop late in the season, taking over for Ray Oyler, a slick fielder who batted only .135 for the year. People remained skeptical that the Tigers would make such a drastic move in the World Series, but Smith was bold enough, and impressed enough by Stanley—and maybe badgered enough by Cash—to pull the trigger.

The new look was described by Curt Gowdy, the NBC announcer, as "the Gibson lineup." To me, though, it was the Kaline lineup. Or the Oyler-less lineup, which was just as meaningful. I'd made a nice living against eight-hole hitters. In a normal game, I'd get about eight strikeouts, and maybe five of them would be divided up between the opposing pitcher and the guy batting eighth. Without Oyler in the order, the Tigers didn't really have a traditional number-eight hitter. For me, that stunk.

Though not an exceptional hitter, Stanley was a capable one, and I watched with interest as my curveball navigated toward the outside corner and the Tigers' new shortstop read it wrong. I'd thrown the curve uncharacteristically well in my last start, the 1–0 shutout of Houston, and the feel for it seemed to be sticking around, suggesting that more of those might be in order for a while. There weren't many games in which I gave the batters a lot of looks at my curve—as a rule, it was a pretty shabby pitch, to tell the truth—but when I did, the majority came early. In the late innings, when my energy was sapped, the curveball was harder to command and reprimanded me by hanging in the wrong places. That was especially true on hot days like this one. I'd only thrown seven pitches, and sweat was already rolling down my face. My long sleeves might have had something to do with that, but I never took the mound without them, regardless of the weather. I preferred to keep the heat in; didn't want my arm to cool off. Besides, I liked sweat. It had its advantages. But I knew that, on this particular afternoon, because of the heat and the pressures of the World Series, the late innings were going to be a challenge, which meant my curveball would have a short shelf life. I committed to it early, while it still had some snap.

Even so, I didn't ordinarily use it against right-handed batters. The World Series, though, has a way of encouraging a little something different. I'd found that out the previous October. Boston's scouting report said that I didn't have much of a curve or slider, and I struck out a lot of Red Sox on breaking pitches they couldn't come to terms with. At the same time, though, you can't forget what brought you to the dance. *Our* scouting report urged me not to throw Carl Yastrzemski a high fastball. Really? High fastballs were my meal ticket, and I damn sure wasn't going to hold them back against the Triple Crown winner of the American League, no matter what he'd done to other people's. When I elevated four-seamers for Yaz in game one, he popped three of them up. It was the same story against Harmon Killebrew, albeit a strikeout, in the ninth inning of the 1965 All-Star Game, with the tying run on second base, and against Sadaharu Oh when we toured Japan, three pitches in a row. So much for scouting reports. Against the Red Sox, the book on one player—I forget who—was to work him with change-ups inside. First of all, my change-up was terrible. Secondly, I would *never* throw one inside; not even a *good* one. I might also point out that on the day after Yastrzemski went 0-for-4 against me in 1967, Dick Hughes and Joe Hoerner pitched him in accordance with the scouting report, and he hit two home runs.

The difference in the World Series is not the stage or the stakes, but the fact that you don't have a history with the opponent. There was no interleague play in my day. Most of the teams trained in Florida—our camp in St. Petersburg was just over an hour away from Detroit's in Lakeland, and we played the Tigers every year—but you can't learn much from exhibition games. For me, the World Series, more than any other occasion, was about pitching on the fly. On the afternoon of October 2, 1968, that translated into a few more curveballs than usual. After Mickey Stanley's reaction to my first one, I was convinced.

It's said that pitchers who throw extremely hard tend to have good curveballs, due to their arm speed and the spin they can generate. Sandy Koufax, Nolan Ryan, and Dwight Gooden attested to that. I had the speed and the spin, but my curve was good only sometimes. The first one of the day suggested that this was one of those times. My slider, by contrast, was good more often than not. This day, however, early indications were inconclusive. My second slider of the day, like the first, sailed outside. It was better-placed and more tempting than the previous one, but Stanley resisted.

All year, I'd been able to home in on that outside corner, in particular, but when I missed it again, this time with a two-seam fastball, I was behind in the count and flirting with my old first-inning gremlin. To fight it off, I had to go back to what was working.

I got the slider sign from McCarver, gripped the seam, and broke off another curveball. It, too, was low and outside, but Stanley, still expecting anything but that, bailed out, swung tentatively, and missed badly.

A four-seam fastball was now in order. I didn't want to extend the count to 3-and-2. My heart wasn't set on a strikeout, but I'd be glad to have one, and the high heater had always been generous in that respect. This one was a good pitch, but Stanley fouled it back with a swing that wasn't lusty enough to discourage another.

For the fastball to follow, McCarver held his mitt on the outer edge of the strike zone and just below Stanley's waist. That way, I could use the target for either the two- or four-seamer. I went with the two-seamer, but once again it tailed low and outside. I had failed to avoid the full count.

At this point, the call was more difficult. With Kaline and Norm Cash behind him, I had no interest in walking Stanley. The inability to locate my fastball on the outside corner, the spot that for six months had been my own personal property, made me reluctant to come back with another one. The curveball was serving me best, but it was not yet a pitch in which I placed my faith in times of trouble. Meanwhile, I was determined to throw my first good slider of the day.

I was proud of my slider. Until 1959, when I spent most of the season with the Cardinals' Triple-A farm club in Omaha, where I grew up, I thought my slider was actually a curveball. At that point, I truly *didn't* have a curveball. The Cardinals' pitching coach, Howard Pollet, taught me how to twist my wrist and pull the ball downward to make it drop; but the pitch wasn't natural for me and it took a long time to make it legitimate; even longer to keep it out of the dirt. I had no such problem with the slider.

With the slider, in fact, *I* had become the mentor. I taught it to Steve Carlton, and there are those who think his slider was unequaled. McCarver, who caught him in St. Louis and later became Lefty's personal catcher in Philadelphia, is one of those. At a dinner in Cooperstown the night before Carlton was inducted into the Hall of Fame, Tim was asked to say a few words about him. He took the microphone and said that if Carl Hubbell goes down in history as having the best screwball and Sandy Koufax goes down as having the best curveball and Nolan Ryan goes down as having the best fastball, Carlton will be remembered as having the best slider the game has ever seen. Afterward, when everybody was milling around, I worked my way through the crowd, got in Tim's face, and said, "The best *left-handed* slider! Carlton had the best *left-handed* slider!" Yeah, I was proud of my slider. And with a 3-2 count on Mickey Stanley, I needed to get it right.

I didn't. Preoccupied with keeping it in the strike zone, I hung it. High and over the middle of the plate. Stanley slapped it into left field for a single. Given the quality of the pitch, it was the best I could hope for.

———

YOU WOULD THINK that, by 1968, I'd have some sense of Al Kaline as a hitter. He was in his sixteenth season—the man had won the American League batting title in 1955 at the mind-boggling age of twenty—and I was in my tenth. He'd been an All-Star thirteen times and I'd been selected five. He was the greatest Tiger since Ty Cobb. But I'd never thrown him a pitch. Except in spring training, for what that's worth. Which is not much.

In fact, I'd pitched against him—I think—late that spring. April 5, to be exact. Forgive me for not recalling the particulars of our matchup, if we had one. I was a little distracted that day. The night before, Martin Luther King had been murdered in Memphis.

The assassination occurred early in the evening, and I'd over-heard something about it. Not sure what to believe, I hurried over to Lou Brock's room. Orlando Cepeda was with him, and the TV was on. "It's true," Lou said. In my grief and anger—I might have the order wrong there—I couldn't help thinking back two months earlier, when I'd walked past Dr. King in the Atlanta airport. I'd looked him at him and he'd looked back with what seemed to be recognition, but neither of us said any-thing. I wish I had.

At the ballpark the next day, Tim McCarver could see how distraught I was. He was well aware of how strongly I felt about the work Dr. King was doing—Tim and I often talked about race relations—and approached me to offer consolation. He said, "I understand how you feel as a minority, because I was brought up a Catholic in Tennessee, and Tennessee is only six percent Catholic."

"No, Tim," I told him, "you don't understand. You can't. You're white."

He said, "You know, you're right." And that was the end of the conversation.

Our talks usually lasted longer than that. Sometimes, when I vented about bias and attitudes and double standards and subtle discrimination, Tim would point out that people can change. On that score, he spoke from experience. He was a living example of it.

I won't get into specifics about the racial consciousness that McCarver brought to professional baseball as a teen-aged hotshot. Suffice to say that, coming from the South as he did, Tim was very noticeable in that way to not only me but a lot of the Cardinals, black and white. Our team, as a whole, had no tolerance for ethnic or racial disrespect. We'd talk about it openly and in no uncertain terms. In our clubhouse, nobody got a free pass. But of those who required some talking to, few entertained the subject as sincerely as McCarver.

From the beginning, he was kind of a pet project of mine. In our first big-league camp together, we were boarding the bus after an exhibition game in Bradenton and McCarver was eating an ice cream cone. The way he remembers it, he was drinking an orange soda; but this is my book, so it's an ice cream cone. Anyhow, I gave Curt Flood a little nudge and said, "Hey, Tim, can I have a bite of that?" He looked at me, looked at Curt, stuttered for a second, and said, "I'll, uh, save you some." Flood and I broke up.

I'll confess to being the leading agitator in the Cardinals' adamant—you could say aggressive—stance on race. If a teammate made any distinctions based on color, my practice was to confront him, let him know how we felt about it as a ball club, and give him every chance to change. Tim did, quickly and completely. It wasn't too long before he was like a brother to me; and still is. Maybe the best memento we share is the photograph that appeared in the New York *Daily News* after game five of the 1964 World Series, the occasion of my first World Series victory. I pitched ten innings against that great lineup—Mickey Mantle, Roger Maris, Elston Howard, Joe Pepitone, and the rest— and gave up just a couple unearned runs. Struck out 13. It was probably the greatest game of my life to that point, but we won it only because McCarver, all of twenty-two years old at the time, hit a three-run homer in the top of the tenth. The photo shows us in the clubhouse afterward, with me puckering up to give Tim—looking sharp in his crew cut, I might add—a big kiss on the cheek.

Of course, having a relationship like that left me at liberty to give him hell about anything and everything. At the top of the list was his throwing. In addition to being a fine hitter, McCarver was a terrific receiver and the best I've ever known at thinking with his pitcher; but he couldn't throw a lick. And yet, when a fast runner reached first base, he would invariably plod out to the mound, knowing I hated that, and say, "All right, now, give me a shot at him." I'd laugh and say, "Tim, *I* had a shot at the guy and didn't get him. What do you think *you're* gonna do?" Or, "I don't have time to be watching him for you. And you're not gonna throw him out anyway." The visit almost always ended with, "Just get the hell back there and catch."

So imagine my surprise when, on the first pitch to Kaline—a swinging strike on a low fastball—McCarver threw out Stanley trying to steal second base. Quick release, right on the money to Javier. Stanley got up and kicked the bag on his way to the dugout. Loved it. Go get 'em, Tim!

———

LIKE ME, KALINE had broken into the headlines as a high school basketball player. Growing up in a working-class neighborhood in Baltimore, he'd been the first one in his family to finish high school. But while I took my basketball game to Creighton University, Kaline signed with the Tigers for enough money to make him a "bonus baby," which meant that, according to the rules of the day, he had to stick with the big-league team for two years. In most instances, bonus babies learned the game by watching the veterans for those two years, maybe got to the plate from time to time, when it didn't matter much, or tossed a few meaningless innings to get the general sense of it, and were then packed off to the minors to get started on their careers. Kaline never made it to the minor leagues. By his second season, he was Detroit's starting right fielder. That was the year before he won the batting title by hitting .340.

In 1968, notwithstanding his broken arm and limited playing time, he once again led the Tigers in hitting. It was only .287, but .301 got Yastrzemski the batting crown that season. Kaline also hit enough home runs in '68 to pass Hank Greenberg as the team's all-time leader. Willie Horton said he regarded Kaline as the club's Abraham Lincoln.

I was pretty sure that Lincoln couldn't catch up with my four-seamer, and was interested to see how Kaline played out in that respect. For all his accomplishments, he was a batter I intended to challenge. Not because of his age, necessarily, or his health, and certainly not out of overconfidence in the matchup. It was because he was right-handed.

For the most part, I didn't fret too much over right-handed

hitters. I made an exception for Henry Aaron, and eventually settled for showing him curves or off-speed sliders and letting him smash the ball against our shortstop's shins. But Mays, Clemente, Banks . . . I'm not saying those guys couldn't and wouldn't hurt me now and again; it's just that I had more to worry about from Willie McCovey, Willie Stargell, Billy Williams, or even a left-handed annoyance like Ron Fairly or Willie Davis. *Ed Kranepool,* for crying out loud.

The right-left dynamic is an old, familiar story. It's one of the principles behind platoons and pinch hitters. I guess it's a matter, for the most part, of a speeding baseball being easier to step into and hit when it's moving toward you rather than away from you; approaching from right in front of your eyes instead of the back side of your head. In my case, though, there was an additional factor. My philosophy of pitching was predicated on the out-side corner. With a right-handed hitter at the plate, the outside corner was my glove side. With a left-handed hitter, it was my ball side. I simply had better control to the glove side. Much better. Against a right-handed hitter, I could pitch on my terms. Against a lefty, it was an ongoing negotiation.

So Kaline would be seeing fastballs to start with. After get-ting ahead of him with one—that was my usual MO—and en-joying the sight of the base runner being wiped out by McCarver's throw, I was back to the windup and energized. That called for another fastball; but my command of the corner failed me again. Low and away. So low and away that McCarver let it skip by and grabbed a new ball from the umpire, Tom Gorman.

Apparently, Tim had seen enough of the fastball for the time being. I was more stubborn than that, and, as always, expected him to be in my head. He usually was; but not this time. I shook him off. Actually, it wasn't a shake-off as much as a little turn of the head and raising of the eyes, a "Huh? You want *that*?" It always surprised me when McCarver didn't call for the pitch I was intending to throw. Once, with the bases loaded, I started into my windup as Tim put down his sign, and when I saw it— and it wasn't what I'd anticipated—I was so discombobulated that I balked in a run. I'd learned to take it slower and let him try a different finger. He complied, I nodded, the four-seamer came in above the belt, and Kaline fouled it back.

Now I was ready for McCarver's slider. I was so enthused about it, in fact, and so eager for a big, sharp break that would overmatch the Tigers' icon and put the rest of them on the defensive, that I overthrew the damn thing, high, ball two. I hadn't found my groove yet. Hadn't found my slider, either. That wouldn't do.

I gave it another shot. It was my best slider so far—not the curveball that Curt Gowdy called—darting to the outside corner and dropping to the knee. Kaline swung at it, my teammates headed for the dugout, and Tim rolled the ball back for Denny McLain.

THE NIGHT BEFORE game one, while I was taking it easy at my summer home in St. Louis with my wife (at the time), Charline, and older daughter, Renee, who was playing hooky from her school in Omaha, Denny McLain was at a local nightclub entertaining, as he often did—when he wasn't bowling (at one point, he evidently averaged over 200 in several leagues) or flying his plane to Las Vegas—on the organ. His selections included "Sweet Georgia Brown," which he dedicated to the former Globetrotter whom he'd be opposing the following afternoon.

It was hard for me to imagine the pace he kept up. I suppose that explained why he drank up to twenty bottles of Pepsi a day and kept a glass of it on his nightstand. McLain, it seemed, never slowed down, and he had no intention of doing so when the extra-long season was over. He had a two-week Vegas gig all lined for just after the Series, sharing a lounge with Shecky Greene. While he was dazzling the audience with "The Girl from Ipanema," I'd be tinkering on our house in Omaha, putting model cars together, listening to jazz records, and maybe strumming a few easy chords on my ukulele. We were, needless to say, different. McLain wore a mink coat *in the minor leagues.* I didn't have mink-coat money until I'd won the seventh game of a World Series. McLain had a phone in his car. He hustled people on the golf course. He hung around with Glen Campbell and Tommy Smothers. If he was being interviewed and the reporter's pen ran out of ink, Denny would hand him another one.

For all of that, there were a few similarities between McLain and me. We'd both grown up in the Midwest; Denny was from the Chicago area. We'd both had baseball drilled into us by strong family members—in my case, my older brother Josh; in his, his father. We were both right-handed power pitchers. We both liked to throw our fastballs up in the strike zone. But while McLain craved winning, I don't believe he detested losing—or giving up a run—nearly as much as I did. As great as he was in 1968, McLain led the American League in home runs allowed for the third straight year, and getting taken out of the ballpark never seemed to faze him. He purposely let Mickey Mantle hit one.

That was the occasion of his 31st win. It was the eighth inning, the pennant had been clinched, and the Tigers were up 6–1. Mantle, at the time, was tied with Jimmie Foxx for third place on the major-league home run list, behind Babe Ruth and Willie Mays. Mickey was a favorite of his, and McLain had told the Tigers' catcher, Jim Price, to alert him that the ball would be floating up there soft and fat. After lobbing up a cookie on the first pitch, which Mantle, reluctant to believe what he'd heard, just gawked at, McLain motioned with his hand that another one like it would follow. Mantle fouled it off, then backed out of the batter's box and stared at McLain, who indicated that one more was coming. Mantle crushed that one into the upper deck. I liked Mickey, too—who didn't?—but I couldn't conceive of any possible circumstance or sentiment that would persuade me to lay one in there, with generosity aforethought, for him or anyone else. I made the comment at the time that I would drop my pants on the mound before I'd defer that way to an opposing player. It was simply not in my DNA. Home runs, literally—along with losing—kept me up at night.

I suspect that some of Denny's teammates questioned the Mantle incident. They questioned a lot of things involving McLain. It was public knowledge that they had issues with what they perceived as the special treatment he received from Mayo Smith and the Tigers. From their perspective, McLain wasn't held to the team rules that applied to everyone else. While the rest of the club traveled together, McLain often flew his private plane. He regularly left the ballpark early after pitching, and the other players might not see him again until a couple hours before his next start. Once, after McLain had beaten the Yankees on a two-run homer by Kaline—whose style, as opposed to McLain's, was to not concern himself with style—the writers crowded around the self-promoting pitcher, as usual, and one of them remarked to Kaline, sitting alone, that his big blow must have been a mirage, since nobody was asking him about it. "No,"

Kaline replied, "it's just that I'm around all the time. You don't get a chance to talk to Denny much."

That was pretty much the way I'd have responded to a guy like McLain—with a kind of edgy humor. I didn't know him well, of course, but from what I could piece together, he reminded me a bit of Dick Allen, who would later be my teammate for one season. Allen showed up late for ball games and spring training, and he didn't jump through the same hoops that everybody else did, but I had no problem with him because, like McLain, he delivered in a big way. Great players can be rare birds, and sometimes you just have to let them do their own thing. When Dick Allen drove in 100 runs for us, I was damn glad to have him on the ball club.

McLain's lifestyle would ultimately catch up with him, in the form of suspensions—one relating to gambling, another to carrying a handgun on a team flight—and, later, jail, on a variety of charges. He was out of the big leagues by the time he was twenty-nine. But in the late sixties, he was as celebrated, and certainly as successful, as any pitcher in the game, averaging nearly 22 victories a year over a period of five seasons.

In 1968, McLain had been not only his league's Cy Young Award winner—an honor he'd claim again the next year—but its MVP, as well. We had *that* in common.

THE AMERICAN LEAGUE had nobody quite like Lou Brock. Oakland's shortstop, Bert Campaneris, was a premier base stealer and an excellent player, but he didn't create the ruckus that Brock did in the course of a ball game, or score as many runs, or hit for as much average or power. Lou was special, and as the Red Sox found out in 1967, he was extra-special under pressure. The aspect of his nature that allowed him to steal so many bases, in addition to his obvious speed, was the instinct he possessed to take advantage of every moment and opportunity; and there was no moment or opportunity like a World Series. Brock had devastated Boston: a .414 average, two doubles, a home run, and a record seven stolen bases. In game one alone, he piled up four hits and a pair of steals. I was happy to have the Corvette that came with winning the Series MVP award—even though I'd sold the one I received in 1964—but truthfully I thought Brock deserved it more. So did a radio station in St. Louis, and it presented him a car of his own choosing. That, too, was an opportunity Lou took full advantage of, requesting a swanky Cadillac Eldorado.

The trade that brought Brock to St. Louis, in June of 1964, was a turning point in Cardinal history. At the time, though, I frankly didn't care for it. In Brock's few years with the Cubs, I hadn't found it difficult to get him out, even though he was a left-handed hitter. He seemed tentative, and looked the same in the outfield. The Cardinals were in the market for an outfielder to replace Stan Musial, who retired at the end of the 1963 season, but I suspected that the deal would cause more problems than it solved. It involved three players each way, and included, from our side, Ernie Broglio, an accomplished right-handed pitcher who was my age and had, like me, won 18 games the year before, with a better earned run average than mine. Broglio was considered our ace. With his departure, I inherited that role, and while I didn't believe the trade was good for the ball club, I appreciated what it did for my confidence.

With Johnny Keane as the manager, the Cardinals, in fact, had a way of bringing out the best in promising, underachieving, mishandled players. Lou, a country kid from Arkansas who had played college ball at Southern University, was a very smart, very sensitive guy with a tendency to think and worry himself into knots. He was also enormously strong. Just before the Polo Grounds were torn down, he'd become the first player ever to hit a ball over the 483-foot sign in dead center field. But even so, the Cubs had wanted him to slap the ball around the diamond, like Richie Ashburn of the Phillies, and get on base for Billy Williams, Ernie Banks, and Ron Santo. Brock didn't steal many bases in Chicago. Keane, however, urged him to shake off his burdens and cut loose, both at bat and on the base paths. In the exhilaration of just being himself, Lou energized our club almost immediately, batting .348 the rest of the season.

In 1968, he had started slowly before getting it together to lead the National League in doubles, triples, and of course stolen bases for the third straight year on the way to eight out of nine. And now, as stepped onto the big stage to lead off the bottom of the first inning, I fully expected Brock—the best money player I'd ever seen—to make Denny McLain miserable.

McLain, pitching in short sleeves, wore his cap high on his head, with the bill pulled down like an awning over his eyes, and while my delivery was fast and furious, his was deliberate and smooth. He raised his hands behind his head, lifted his left leg, straightened it to the height of his eyes, and delivered the ball—most of the time—from directly over the top.

Brock was a first-pitch hitter, but McLain's opening fastball was too high for his liking or Tom Gorman's. There had been speculation, going in, that McLain might be at a disadvantage with a National League umpire behind the plate. National League umps wore their chest protectors under their coats, and they squatted down low, peering from the side of the catcher's head. Pitches around the upper edge of the strike zone were likely to appear high from their perspective. American League umpires wore bigger chest protectors outside their coats and stood straighter, directly behind and looking over the catcher, which made them more sympathetic to high strikes. Gorman was a National League ump, and McLain was a high-ball pitcher.

The theory made sense, but I didn't feel sorry for McLain. I depended on the high strike, too, and besides that, my history with Tom Gorman wasn't the happiest. There was one particular game in which he'd been giving me a hard time—a *really* hard time—and when I stepped up to bat I brought along an attitude, which didn't improve when the first pitch came in high, I let it pass, and Gorman said, "Strike one."

I said, "Tom, that ball was high."

He didn't respond. Then, when the next pitch resembled the first: "Strike two."

"Tom," I said, "that pitch was high, and if you're going to call it a strike when I'm batting I want the same pitch when I'm out there on the mound."

He said, "Yeah, well, go ahead and take it again."

I swung at the next one, returned to my seat, and when I went back to the mound he still wasn't giving me the high strike.

For the most part, though, the National League strike zone didn't trouble me. The way my fastball rode, it appeared to rise, and hitters tended to swing at it. I didn't need to count on the umpire, and I figured that McLain wouldn't, either. The Cardinals were a high-fastball-hitting team.

Behind in the count, McLain surprisingly followed with a curveball—a pitch he'd folded into his repertoire a couple years before—and Brock was out in front of it. Then a fastball buzzed inside, just off Lou's hip. When the high fastball returned, up around the shoulders, Brock chopped it to Stanley, which seemed like a good place to go. With Lou running, a bouncing ball to shortstop was never a certain out. But Stanley showed no signs of being a center fielder, and his throw reached Norm Cash in the nick of time.

On the air, Harry Caray wondered if Brock had purposely tested Stanley right off the bat. Believe me, Lou Brock would never hit a ball directly at *anybody*. We couldn't even get him to bunt.

FOR ALL OUR problems scoring runs, I thought the Cardinals had the best one-two hitters in the business. Curt Flood was the soul of our ball club. I might be a little biased, because Curt was my best friend on the team, but in my estimation he was the quintessential Cardinal—intelligent, funny, caring, selfless, and a hell of a player.

His reputation had been built mostly on speed and his brilliant defense in center field, but Curt was a consistent .300 hitter who, in 1968, had led the team at .301. Even more impressive, he was able to do that while consistently drawing out the count to give Brock a chance to steal second base, often putting himself in a two-strike hole. Curt was also very adept at moving Lou over to third by hitting the ball to the right side, and always willing to do it, even though it typically meant giving himself up. It was a tremendous feat to bang out 200 hits—he led the league with 211 in 1964—while doing all the team-first things required of a good two-hole hitter with a great base stealer in front of him. He made Brock better, made the hitters behind him better, and made the rest of us better, too.

I believe that Curt's mastery of situational baseball actually made him a more proficient hitter overall. Although he batted right-handed and crowded the plate, a high percentage of his hits fell into right field, and a high percentage of *those* came on inside pitches, which is uncommon. He had a knack for pulling the handle through an inside strike—they call it an inside-out swing—to angle the bat and hit the ball where it hadn't been pitched.

Hitting to the opposite field was a skill I'd always admired. I don't know if Flood learned it from Dick Groat, a former team-mate who excelled at it, but they used the same method—hands in, so the bat head doesn't get out in front of the ball. At one point, Groat, at my request, walked me through the process. When I posed the same question to Stan Musial, though, the reply was a little different. Stan wasn't much for explaining. I happened to be standing behind the batting cage one day when Musial, the greatest left-handed hitter in the history of the National League, was in the box being Musial, and I took the opportunity to ask, "Stan, how do you hit the ball to left field that well?"

He looked at me, turned back to the pitcher, and said, "Like this!" Whap. Whap. Whap. About five line drives in a row, bullets to left field. Stan couldn't tell you how he did what he did—he'd just show you and laugh.

Flood was also unusually good at checking his swing. He'd often take a short, pretty good hack at the ball, then quickly—and Curt was *quick*—pull the bat back behind his head. More times than not, the umpire would call it a ball. And that's what happened on McLain's first pitch to him, a high curveball. Bill Freehan, the Tigers' catcher, didn't even ask Gorman to consult the first-base umpire about whether Flood had offered at the ball. It wasn't the custom then. In today's game, that would have been strike one.

Curt took a bigger swing at McLain's next delivery, the calling-card high fastball, and came up empty. When the same pitch came again, he foul-tipped it off Freehan's mitt.

With two strikes now, McLain paced around a bit, his head bowed in thought, fidgeted, stalled, wound up, and dropped his elbow down for a sidearm fastball, his first of the day. It was a pitch that had recently come into its own for him. This one, however, missed high—by National League standards, anyway—and perhaps inside, which surprised me. I would never throw a sidearm pitch inside to a right-handed batter, because he'd have a tendency to pull away from anything that came out of that arm slot, leaving him vulnerable on the outside corner and dangerous on the inner half. I dropped down infrequently, because my arm wasn't conditioned that way—even when I took ground balls in infield practice, which I liked to do between starts, I'd make sure to throw over the top, to loosen my shoulder—but when I did, it was always to a right-hander, and I always put the ball on the outer part of the plate. Or at least attempted to. When I succeeded, the batter rarely, if ever, reached it.

McLain doubled down on the same angle, located the pitch in the same place, and Flood fouled it off to the right. When he came sidearm for the third straight time, finally zeroing in on the outside corner, Curt lifted the ball into the shadows of right field, where Kaline, drifting to his left through the hot dog wrappers, grabbed it easily for the second out.

WHEN THE CARDINALS traded for Roger Maris prior to the 1967 season, he was considered to be washed up, at thirty-two, and hard to get along with. We found him decidedly neither.

He certainly wasn't the same hitter he'd been in 1961, when

he won the American League MVP award for the second year in a row and broke Babe Ruth's single-season home run record with 61. Age and injuries and New York had beaten him down, sapped his power, and perhaps made him a little grumpy—toward the end of his time with the Yankees he had purchased a plastic hand with the middle finger raised and placed it next to his locker—but power was a commodity we were used to doing without and grumpy was a quality close to my heart. In our clubhouse, Roger fit right in. More important, he was a team player and a fundamentally sound one.

He was also a pleasant guy who took Mike Shannon off our hands. I say that in jest, because Mike was eminently likable, but he was in his own world—we called him Moon Man—and we found it interesting that Maris, so hardened and down-to-earth, would hit it off so well with him. Shannon simply made Roger smile, which is something he hadn't done a lot of in New York. Contrary to what we'd read about him in the papers, Maris wasn't chronically miserable. (Whitey Ford had said that, if he had to put together a cabinet, Roger would be his Secretary of Grievances.) He was just a plainspoken, chain-smoking North Dakotan who was happy to be away from high-rise apartments and the media capital of the universe; and happy to finally be happy.

By World Series time, Maris had already announced that he'd be retiring after the season. His two years with us had been much admired—the man never threw to the wrong base—but modest statistically. Roger was one of the best I'd seen at pulling an outside pitch, a talent that no doubt had served him well at Yankee Stadium, with its short right field. It would have brought him a good many home runs at old Busch Stadium, as well—if you ask me, that right-field pavilion was a menace to society—but the round, cookie-cutter new version, where we moved in 1966, played more fairly, which is to say that it was more of a pitcher's park. Plus, Roger's wrist bothered him.

When Maris spoke, everybody listened, and late in the year, as Detroit was wrapping up the American League pennant and McLain was winning his 30th game, he had said something unexpected that stuck with us. He told us that McLain might not be the Tiger pitcher we really had to worry about. He thought the guy who might give us the most trouble was their heavyset left-hander, Mickey Lolich.

Roger hadn't really crushed McLain in their previous encounters, but he looked confident when he settled into the batter's box with two outs. McLain started him with an overhand curve that swooped toward the inside corner, belt high. It was a pitch that I suspect Maris had deposited on the far side of many a right-field fence. He slashed at it and sent the ball in that direction, but times had changed. The park was big, the wrist was bad, and there was an Anheuser-Busch distributorship waiting for Roger in Florida. Kaline took a couple steps forward, out of the shadows, and brought the first inning to a close.

	1	2	3	4	5	6	7	8	9	R	H	E
Tigers	0									0	1	0
Cardinals	0									0	0	0

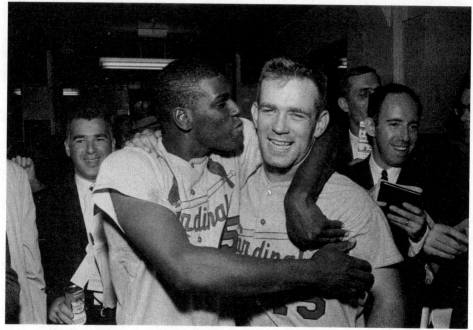

(Copyright Bettmann/Corbis/AP Images)

Although we arrived in St. Louis from profoundly different backgrounds, McCarver and I grew closer every year. On the day in 1964
when he clubbed a three-run, tenth-inning homer to beat the Yankees
in New York and present me with my first-ever World Series victory,
Tim became my new best friend. We still treasure this photo.

Second Inning

THE POMP AND circumstance had stepped aside, thank goodness. The sun was bearing down from the direction of the right-field corner, pointing my shadow toward third base, which I had every intention of keeping vacant. The sweat was rolling off my chin and down my wrists, the way I liked it. Having muddled through the first inning, I now had a mandate and a suitable working environment for the second. It was time to settle in and find the corners. The big boys were coming to bat.

The first of them was Norm Cash, the Tigers' cleanup hitter, first baseman, and class clown. A former football player—he'd been drafted by the Chicago Bears as a running back—Cash was a hard-living, late-night guy, the life of bars and parties, the kind who would have felt right at home with the old Yankees of Mantle, Ford, and Billy Martin. In the off-season, he and his teammate, Gates Brown, the Tigers' best pinch hitter, took their comedy routine on the banquet circuit. He had himself a good time at the ballpark, as well. Once, when Nolan Ryan was working on a no-hitter, Cash walked to the plate with a table leg. In his Texas drawl, he carried on colorful conversations with runners at first base. He got some laughs with his on-field imitations of Emmett Ashford, the animated umpire. He also hit.

Cash's best season had been 1961. As Maris overtook Ruth and lost clumps of his hair, Cash, practically unnoticed, led the American League with a .361 batting average, whacking 41 home runs and driving in 132 runs in the process. With the exception of the 39 homers he hit the following season, he never again approached those numbers. Years later, he admitted that he'd corked his bat in '61, drilling an eight-inch hole in the end of it. But he remained a consistent power threat, and the Tiger that concerned me the most. Detroit's other ranking sluggers—Kaline, Willie Horton, and Bill Freehan—batted right-handed, and for that reason I liked my odds against them. McAuliffe and Jim Northrup gave the lineup some left-handed balance, and their power had to be respected, but Cash was the guy best equipped to beat me with a big swing. I was pleased to see him leading off the inning, with nobody to drive in but himself.

Since my curveball had served me well in the first, and since I'd most likely be leaving it behind in the later innings, and since World Series scouting reports always seemed to focus on my fastball, which I appreciated, I started Cash with a big, off-speed breaking pitch that approached from the outside edge and dropped in for called strike one. It wasn't a pitch I often threw when I was just trying to get ahead of the hitter—in fact, it wasn't a pitch that I often threw *at all*, because, unlike the back-door slider that McCarver had coaxed out of me that year, I couldn't spot it very well and was generally content just to get the thing over the plate, preferably around the knees—but sometimes you just have to go with the currents of the game. I also had the element of surprise on my side. On most days, that was the best thing about my curveball.

I followed with my customary fastball away, and the corner eluded me again.

It was still essential that, with my fastball, I stake a claim to the outer part of the plate. But that requires more than just fastballs on the outer part of the plate. To pitch outside, you have to pitch *inside*. Let me amend that. You have to *come* inside. Pitching inside implies placing the ball in the strike zone, which isn't something you want to do a lot of. *Coming* inside is not about throwing strikes. The purpose is to bring the ball inside often enough, and aggressively enough, to keep the batter from striding confidently across the plate to the side that you positively have to command; to keep him honest, in other words.

My dedication to that reality had earned me a reputation. I'd been called a headhunter, a knockdown artist, a mean son of a bitch, you name it. I was, in fact, none of those things. I was simply a competitor who understood the need to keep a dangerous batter in his place and wasn't timid about satisfying that requirement. If, in the bargain, the batter happened to get himself hit, he had nothing to complain about. He was awarded first base, after all. I hadn't known a hell of a lot about pitching when I came to the big leagues, but I knew you had to come inside to pitch outside and occasionally, as part of the game, there was collateral damage. Every pitcher knew that much. Every hitter, too, if he had any sense.

There had been a game in 1961—my second start of my first full season with the Cardinals—when Duke Snider, the Dodgers' great outfielder and left-handed power hitter, had taken away my outside corner. Snider was normally a dead pull hitter, but the first time up he waded into an outside fastball and slashed it hard to third base. The next time, with two runners on, I gave him another fastball away, and he dove across the plate and poked it into the ridiculously close left-field seats at Los Angeles Coliseum. That was enough. The third time he came up, I bored a four-seamer inside, intent on reclaiming what was rightfully mine. It broke his arm. Snider, by that time, was a highly respected veteran, and I was a kid nobody, so after the game I waited for him by the Dodgers' clubhouse. I told him I was sorry about his arm; I hadn't meant to hit him. He smiled and said he knew that, don't worry about it; he had it coming. I don't believe I ever again apologized to an active player.

In fact, I once went to dinner with my old teammate and friend Bill White after a game in which I nailed him on the same principle, and he received no apology. Before he was traded to the Phillies in 1966, White had been a bedrock player for the Cardinals. He loved that pavilion roof behind right field in old Busch Stadium and, as a left-handed hitter strong as an ox, made it his business to pull every pitch he possibly could, inside or out. On outer-half fastballs, Bill lunged so recklessly across the plate that I'd given him fair warning: I said that, if he ever got traded and did that to me, he would have a close encounter with the subsequent pitch. It took three years—even though he clubbed a big home run against me the first time we faced each other—but in July of 1968, Bill stepped brazenly into an outside fastball of mine and pulled it down the right-field line, then fended off the next one with his elbow. On his way to first base he called me crazy, and just for emphasis he repeated the charge over dinner. But the way I saw it, *he* was the crazy one. I'd told him what would happen, and he'd damn well known I meant it. Or should have, being a smart guy.

As much as I believed in throwing inside on a regular basis, it was a bit of a risk to do it to Cash on a 1-1 count. Margin of error. When I crowded a power hitter, I was willing to err on the body side of the corner but not the plate side. A lot of modern pitchers, on the other hand, have embraced the need to pitch inside without respecting the perils of it. They're trying to throw inside *strikes*, which is asking for trouble. An outside strike, which very few hitters can put over the fence, is much more effective than an inside strike; but an inside *ball*—especially a fastball— is much more effective than an outside ball. When home runs proliferated around the turn of the century, I was of the opinion that the inside strike was every bit as responsible as steroids and small ballparks.

My immediate problem, consequently, was that I wanted to come inside to Cash, but another ball would put me behind in the confrontation. So, in the interest of a strike and defiance of my usual MO, I permitted myself to challenge him and trust my four-seamer. I'd hoped, however, that it would catch less of the plate than it did. Fortunately, it had good cutting action. Cash fouled it back.

Seeing that he was slightly under the fastball, I put the next one a little higher and back toward the more familiar corner, where I intended to spend the afternoon if I could only locate it. This one found the spot, finally, on the black at the belt, and the Tigers' first baseman went down swinging.

FOLLOWING A DOUBLEHEADER with the Yankees the year before, on the Sunday when Detroit broke out in deadly race riots, Willie Horton had left Tiger Stadium in his uniform and hurried over to the neighborhood where he'd been raised in a housing project. His old stomping grounds, whose ins and outs he'd gotten to know as a kid while selling the *Michigan Chronicle*—a newspaper for the city's black community—were at the heart of the uprising. With the streets roiling around him, Horton hopped onto the roof of a car and urged the crowd to break up. The crowd, in turn, urged its favorite left fielder to climb down and go safely home. Horton continued to ask for calm, but there would be none for four days. During that time, the Tigers played no games, Lyndon Johnson called in federal troops, more than two thousand buildings were destroyed, and forty-three people lost their lives.

Horton had a stake in Detroit; and Detroit had one in him, as well. In the off-season, he sought out troubled young people in the city's projects, tenement buildings, and taverns, offering counsel and inspiration. In-season, he was a rallying point for the black community. The Tigers had been slow to integrate, and Willie had been their first bona fide African American star.

The team's racial makeup, however, hadn't stopped him from loving it for as long as he could remember. When Horton was a teenager, he worked odd jobs in the Tigers' clubhouse. Before that, he and his friends would sneak into Briggs Stadium, as it was called at the time, by following trucks through the service entrance and hiding in dumpsters until the coast was clear. Once, when they were caught, Rocky Colavito, a slugging outfielder who was actually playing for Cleveland at the time, asked if they could be released into his care. When Colavito was later traded to the Tigers, Willie had himself a hero. Ironically, Colavito was ultimately traded away from Detroit to make room for Horton.

Squatty and immensely powerful—he reminded a lot of people of the great Roy Campanella—Horton hit 29 home runs and drove in more than 100 runs in his first full season, which was 1965, and kept up the pace. During that raging summer of '67, he homered in seven straight games, every last one a blast. In '68, he reached his career high with 36 long balls, which of course led the team and trailed only Frank Howard in the American League. His .285 average, believe it or not, ranked fourth in the league. Detroit fans were known to stand and cheer when Horton trotted out to take his position in left field.

Apparently, Mayo Smith felt the same way about Willie. When Horton once crashed into the left-field fence and crumpled to the ground, Smith was in such a hurry to get to his big man that he pulled a muscle on the way out. Poor Mayo. Another time, he ran out to second base when Horton got into a tussle with Ron Hansen of the White Sox, and Willie accidentally stepped on the skipper's toe, sending him limping back to the dugout.

I'm not sure how Ron Hansen came out of that dustup, but Horton was not a guy to trifle with. There's a certain amount of fighting that goes along with being the youngest of twenty-one kids, and yet, that wasn't enough for Willie. He had also been successful in Golden Gloves boxing until his father saw him on television and put an end to that. No problem; he just took the battle to the ball field. The original meeting between Horton and the Detroit catcher, Bill Freehan, might have been the occasion of a Little League all-star game, when Willie crashed into Freehan—who was rugged enough to start at defensive end for Michigan as a sophomore—and the two burly boys proceeded to roll around in the dirt. Like most of the Tigers, Horton had remained a scrapper. In '68, on the day after Kaline's arm was broken, Northrup was beaned by an Oakland pitcher and it was go time. Northrup charged the mound. Eddie Mathews, a veteran brawler, decked the pitcher. Horton, who had chronic problems with tendons and bone spurs in his ankles and legs, was in the whirlpool at the time, and barged onto the field half dressed.

If I'd known about Willie's fondness and aptitude for mixing it up, I might have been more courteous at our first encounter, when he was just breaking into the big leagues. I don't actually remember it, but he tells the story of making the trip to an exhibition game against the Cardinals when he wasn't required to, for the express purpose of getting my autograph. He apparently approached me while I was shagging fly balls before the game, introduced himself as an outfielder, and watched me turn and walk away. I don't doubt the story, because I'd done pretty much the same to Gene Clines and Dave Winfield when they were just starting out. I happened to be an ardent supporter of the no-fraternization rule. I didn't even talk to my teammates at All-Star Games if I didn't have to. As a pitcher on the prowl for any and every competitive edge, I thought it best to stay wrapped in a cloak of mystery; make 'em wonder what was going on in my head. Nor did I care to encourage second thoughts about pitching a guy the way I needed to pitch him. The way I saw it, nothing good could come from consorting with the enemy, who was anybody with a bat and a different-colored uniform. Horton's buddy, Gates Brown, told him he was a fool for riding the bus all the way to St. Petersburg, expecting to get the time of day from me. Gates was a wise man. (For what it's worth, Willie finally got his autograph at the 1970 All-Star Game, when he sent a clubhouse kid over to our side with a ball and a pen.)

Almost as much as McLain, and certainly in a very different way, Horton had become a symbol of the '68 Tigers. Because of his love for Detroit and his sensitivity toward the '67 riots—there was practically another one when the Tigers lost the pennant on the last day of the season and the fans demolished seats, tore up the field, and fought with security guards—Willie believed that he and his teammates were on a holy mission in 1968. He certainly played like it. In midseason, he took off on a ferocious tear.

In September, batting in the bottom of the ninth after the Tigers had just tied Oakland—Reggie Jackson had twice put the A's ahead with home runs—he delivered the game-winning hit for McLain's 30th victory (causing McLain to jump up and bang his head on the roof of the dugout).

Our scouting report said that Horton had trouble with the breaking ball low and away. I had to laugh, because *everybody* has trouble with the breaking ball low and away, including pitchers trying to throw one. Dizzy Dean remarked that I would enjoy pitching to Willie because he was a free swinger. Yes, that gave me some options. But it wasn't quite that simple. Horton was strong enough to knock practically any pitch out of the park—when he was sixteen, playing in a high school championship game at Tiger Stadium, he had mashed a ball deep into the seats in right-center field—and he had a sly way of moving around in the batter's box, tweaking his approach to match up with whoever he was trying to hit. He fared well against crafty pitchers like Dave McNally, Jim Kaat, Tommy John, Bill Lee, and Wilbur Wood; but all those guys were lefties. On the other hand, he also had success with the likes of Jim Palmer, who bore some similarities to me, and Bert Blyleven, whose curveball beat the hell out of mine.

Horton tended to stand a little closer to the mound when he was expecting curves, but I doubted he'd do that against me. He'd also shown he could punish an inside fastball, which he wasn't likely to get when I was pitching. My inside fastballs were mainly for gamesmanship and show. The fact is, I didn't trust my control enough on that side of the plate to try to throw them for strikes. Much later, I came to admire Greg Maddux for the way he could run his two-seamer inside on right-handed hitters; but he was a different breed. He could also make it move in a direction—*toward* a right-handed batter—that I couldn't. At any rate, if I brought my fastball high and tight to Willie Horton, it would be a purpose pitch, and not the first to come his way. It was said that Sonny Siebert knocked him down eight times in one game. I don't know if I believed that; but I did believe that Horton had pretty much seen everything there was to see, and handled most of it.

Sometimes, when a batter presents that many complications, the solution is simple. I'd just pitch him my way, pay attention, and go from there.

Fastball on the outside corner.

It had taken an inning or so, but my rhythm was kicking in, which meant that my stuff was now finding its spots. Horton couldn't quite check his swing. As he went around, I found it interesting that his left shoulder pulled away in a manner that made it impossible for him to reach a pitch in that location. Duly noted. A lot of things were suddenly lining up.

I was working quickly, feeding off momentum, and Willie, sensing it, wanted to stem the tide. He stepped out of the box for a moment, adjusted the batting glove on his left hand—like most players of the day, he wore only one—stepped back in, signaled to the umpire that he wasn't ready, smoothed the dirt, signaled to the umpire that he was ready, and finally cocked his bat behind his helmet. He was a man ahead of his time.

Having gathered himself, Horton had a legitimate rip at the next fastball, which caught more of the plate than it was supposed to, but he wasn't quite in sync with it and failed to make contact. He might have been ahead of his time, but he was a tick behind the four-seamer.

There were two strikes now, and Horton, mindful that he hadn't been equal to the hard stuff—it didn't surprise me, since he held his hands high and swung a very heavy bat—would have to speed it up a notch. He couldn't afford to set himself for anything but the fastball. Even so, McCarver, liking what he'd seen so far, called for another one. I twitched my head, paused a beat to make sure he understood, and broke off a slow, unexpectedly good curveball that tumbled through the strike zone. Horton stood still, Gorman raised his arm for strike three, and Willie stared curiously at home plate as he walked away, as though he were looking for clues about the very strange thing that had just happened.

THERE WAS NOT much relief from the Tigers' power. They hit 52 more home runs than any other team in either league, and every player in the game one lineup—except McLain, of course—contributed to that number in double figures. These days, that would not be particularly impressive. In the Year of the Pitcher, it surely was.

Batting sixth, for instance, was Jim Northrup, another Michigan native and a former small-college quarterback who had been responsible for 90 RBIs and 21 of Detroit's homers, four of which had been grand slams—three in six days, and two in the same game. Ernie Harwell, the great Tigers announcer, called him the Slammer. His teammates, except for Denny McLain, called him the Grey Fox, for his hair, or Sweet Lips, which was apparently a sarcastic reference to his conversational manner.

McLain called him different things. The two just rubbed each other wrong, openly, especially one night during the season when there was a poker game in another Tiger's room and Northrup took exception to the way McLain played his cards, climbing over the bed to get at him. Of course, that made Northrup an easy target, and McLain punched him in the face before Gates Brown was able to break it up, warning the both of them that there would be no more punching, choking, or robe tearing until the pennant had been won. The period of détente must ultimately have been extended through the World Series, because, while McLain was gracing the organ on the eve of game one, Northrup joined him for a vocal or two.

I'm of the opinion that a little scuffle like that, or even bad blood between a couple players, has little bearing on a ball club as long as the personal stuff stays off the field; and even if it doesn't, it hurts only if one guy undermines another. Besides that, the Tigers, for the most part, were a tight bunch with strong ties from coming up together through the minor leagues. Northrup, Horton, Stanley, and Oyler, in particular, had followed each other around since the early sixties, with several others in close proximity.

More pertinent to me, though, was the synergy of the Tigers' lineup. A batting order like that, with no significant breaks in it, plays harder on a pitcher than one with a couple mega-sluggers and a stretch of ordinary Joes. Without any patsies taking their turns—in this case, not even a light-hitting shortstop—there's no opportunity to ease up and pace yourself. It wears a guy out.

Maybe that's why the '68 Tigers were so prolific in late-inning comebacks. Forty times, they rallied to win games in which they were tied or trailed in the seventh inning or later. Bear in mind, this was not the day of specialty relief pitching. A starter was expected to last more than six innings, and some of us were loath to go less than nine. Against a gauntlet like Detroit's, which had a pitcher stressing and straining over every batter, that was *hard*.

The Tigers made you work. They made the late innings a tough proposition.

That said, the work goes easier when the ball does its part. When I'd returned to the mound, it seemed to suddenly remember that this was 1968. As it had all year—actually, since September of 1967, when I was restored to active duty after Roberto Clemente had shattered my lower leg with a line drive—it was leaping out of my hand and flinging itself over the black perimeter of home plate. We had an understanding: I'd just give my little buddy a proper send-off, and he'd do the rest. With that worked out, I released any tentativeness that I might have started the game with, stopped feeling my way around the strike zone, focused on McCarver, and cut it loose.

The first fastball to Northrup was my best one so far, a called strike at the knees, outside corner.

The Tigers' center fielder didn't fuss and fidget like Horton had after the first strike. Didn't tighten his batting glove or play in the dirt. He stayed in the box, hitched up his belt, pointed his bat a couple times, and whiffed at the next four-seamer, which arrived on the inner half.

I wasn't a champion of wasting a pitch with an 0-2 count. But I wasn't about to serve up a fat strike, either—especially not to a left-handed power hitter. I'd pick a corner and do my best to miss it closely. Since Northrup, a lanky fellow, crowded the plate a bit, and since he had shown himself more likely to swing at a pitch inside than one outside, I came way in with another fastball— too far in to tempt him.

So far, Northrup had seen nothing but fastballs. Through the previous five batters, though, I hadn't let anybody leave the box without a look at something wrinkled; something to bear in mind the next time around. This inning, I'd thrown one breaking ball to Cash, and it was a strike, and one to Horton, and it was a strike. They were both curves.

For Northrup, I chose the backdoor slider. I hadn't thrown a good one yet, but I was feeling it now—feeling the rhythm, the trust, the fourth straight strikeout.

It broke from the outside in, just under Northrup's swing, the ninth strike in the eleven pitches that constituted a very pleasant second inning.

ORLANDO CEPEDA WAS the man with a thousand nicknames. As a kid in Puerto Rico, he was called Paralítico, or the Cripple, in reference to the twisted leg he was born with and carried around until a doctor broke and straightened it. His father, Perucho, was a famous Puerto Rican player known as the Bull, and in deference to him Orlando was referred to as both Peruchin and the Baby Bull. With the Giants, Willie Mays called him Chico. With the Cardinals, Lou Brock called him Mister Charley. His love for Latin music—he played the drums in his own band—led to Cha Cha, and with Cepeda leading the cheers in the clubhouse, the 1967 and '68 Cardinals became known as El Birdos. Borrowing on the Spanish theme, some of us called him Bolillos, which technically refers to white bread but we used in honor of his bowlegs.

He came to us, in exchange for our left-handed pitcher, Ray Sadecki, early in the 1966 season. Cepeda had been a force in San Francisco—a National League home run and RBI champion who made six straight All-Star teams—but he'd been out with a knee injury for most of the 1965 season, and although he was in good shape for '66, he'd lost his first-base job to Willie

McCovey. Relations between Orlando and his manager, Herman Franks, were frosty, and his last game for the Giants was also the last game at old Busch Stadium. After it, he crossed over to our clubhouse—where Red Schoendienst told him he'd be our first baseman—joined us for the trip to Chicago, homered in his Cardinal debut, then helped us open Busch Memorial, where, about a month later, he became the first player to send a ball into the upper deck. He went on to earn the Comeback Player of the Year award for the National League.

Orlando loved being a Cardinal. For one thing, he was allowed to play his countless Latin records and speak Spanish—although Julian Javier was the only one who could speak it back—in the clubhouse. Those things had been forbidden in San Francisco's. Nor was our clubhouse divided into ethnic cliques like San Francisco's.

His enthusiasm was so evident that Cepeda was widely portrayed as the spirit of El Birdos. He received a lot of attention for the cheerleading he conducted atop a trunk—the one in which we kept our valuables—after every victory, and his pep talks after we lost. For my money, though, his main value to us was not in his personality. Too much is made of personality. The fact is, we already had several cheerleaders on the ball club. Hell, even *I* was a cheerleader on the days I wasn't pitching. We were guys who enjoyed the game; especially when it involved winning. We also enjoyed Cha Cha. But you know what I liked best about him?

His power. Until he arrived, we didn't really have any. Before 1967, when Cepeda unanimously won the National League MVP award, nobody on our team—other than Roger Maris, whose pop was in the distant past—had ever hit as many as 20 home runs in a season. I made no secret of my appreciation for

Cepeda's power. One day in '67, we were in the bus outside the Park Sheraton in New York, ready to leave for a game at Shea Stadium, and Orlando wasn't on board. A bellhop came out to say that he was on his way, but some of the players were grumbling, hollering at the driver to get going. I stood up and said, "We're waiting for Cepeda. The pitchers aren't leaving without him."

Cepeda had hit me pretty well early in our careers—a couple home runs—but I'd shut him down over the previous three seasons. Basically, I'd caught him cheating and made him pay for it. He would start a game standing practically on top of the plate when he batted, and I'd pitch in on his hands so he couldn't get the head of the bat around to the ball. But every time he came up, he'd slide a little farther away. He might wait until I was in my motion and kind of shuffle backward, trying to be inconspicuous. By the late innings he'd be way the hell back there, and I'd thank him with sliders on the outside corner. When he came over to our side, I played it all back for him. Orlando had no idea; he thought he'd been tricking me all that time. He said, "Did you *see* me?" I told him, "Of course I saw you." I couldn't believe that he couldn't believe it.

There was one more reason why I fared well against Cepeda. A batter needed quick hands to get around on my fastball, and although Orlando had those, they lugged a lot of freight. He swung one of the heaviest bats in the game, at least forty ounces and occasionally up to forty-five, which, I think, is roughly what they needed to break through castle doors in the Middle Ages. Once, when Cepeda fell into a slump, Lou Brock and I got to talking about it and decided that, whether he was tired or hurt or just stubborn, he was buckling under the weight of his wood. So we took it upon ourselves to get him some new bats. They were the same make as his, with the same signature and every-thing; but instead of the forty-two ounces he'd been swinging we ordered a batch at thirty-six. Of course, we didn't tell him this. We just placed them in his locker. And he started murdering the ball. Put his slump behind him and carried the club for a little while. He must have finally gotten suspicious or something, because one day he grabbed a bat, marched into the training room, and put it on the scale. When it came up as thirty-six ounces, he huffed and puffed and said, "What's this shit?" Then he gathered up all the new bats and threw them away. We still weren't sure if he was tired or hurt or both—he underwent extra training nearly every day for his chronically troublesome right knee, wearing a leaden shoe that weighed more than twenty pounds—but he'd proved his stubbornness, beyond a doubt.

In '68, Cepeda's production had dropped off considerably over the second half of the season. His bat was sluggish—to my eyes, it got heavier as the year went on—and I figured that Denny McLain would be a tough matchup for him, emphasizing the high fastball as he did. There was also the fact that, during a win-ter league game in Puerto Rico a few years before—probably the only one in which they'd faced each other—McLain had struck out Orlando four times in a row.

The first pitch, sure enough, was a high fastball, but it sailed outside. McLain appeared to be overthrowing, straining to make himself just a little bit better than he'd been in a 31–6 season. It's easy, not wearing his number, to recognize the foolishness in that; but he had never pitched in a World Series before. And he was human; in a lot of ways, more human than most of us. Frankly, the foolishness is in thinking that a player—especially a pitcher, standing smack in the middle of the universe—is *not* affected by his first World Series; or any World Series. I'd been in Denny's position, and even though I'd won five straight Series games, they'd come after a disappointing loss in my first one. And I'd been four years older than McLain was, as he dropped down and came sidearm for the second pitch to Cepeda. It was a swinging strike.

The next fastball was again high and outside, and again McLain chased it with a sidearm version. This time, Cepeda—set up, as usual, in a severely closed stance, his back foot rubbing out the chalk in front of Freehan—tapped it foul off Freehan's shin. Following pitch: same slot, same speed, a little higher, same general result, this time the ball looping back over Freehan's shoulder.

Like Orlando, and like me, McLain was stubborn. The lower arm angle was getting the job done, but his style—his *game*—was over the top. Once more he brought his signature, twelve-o'clock fastball, up in the zone. Cepeda, behind it, fouled it far back into the seats along the first-base line.

Seeing the lateness of Orlando's bat, I would have reached back for another. McLain, however—he must not have been quite as stubborn as I was—returned to the sidearm fastball and produced another foul, the fourth in a row. This one was better timed by Cepeda, with a stronger swing that sent the ball straight back to the screen.

The sidearm motion was settling McLain, putting him in more consistent touch with the strike zone. Cepeda, meanwhile, was hanging in, and the more fastballs he saw from that slot, the more likely it was that he'd solve one and square it. He'd come close on the last pitch. McLain, of course, realized this. He wandered to the front of the mound, turned around, crossed the rubber, and stared out at center field for a moment, as Cepeda stepped away from the plate, reached down, and picked up a pinch of dirt in his right hand, the one without a batting glove. When McLain at last reached a decision, he dropped down for the fifth sidearm pitch of the matchup, only this time he scaled back on the speed, twisting off a curve at the outside corner, which is exactly where I'd put sidearm slop like that, if I had any.

Orlando reached for it and poked an easy fly ball to Northrup, right where McLain had been staring, for the first out.

WHEN HE REMOVED his shin guards, McCarver, believe it or not, could run. He was no Maury Wills, but he had some gap power to go along with his tricky speed, and in 1966 he'd actually led the National League in triples. He was the first catcher to ever do that.

Tim took his hitting seriously, God bless him. I loved that in a teammate. But even so, it wasn't easy to take his *bat* seriously. In terms of what he swung, McCarver was the anti-Cepeda. For at least the early years of his career, he conducted his business with a bat that weighed thirty-two ounces—practically a splinter of Cha Cha's. I should point out that Stan Musial also used a surprisingly light bat, thirty-one ounces with an extremely thin handle. I once asked Stan what would happen if the pitch hit his bat on that fragile handle. He just laughed and said that it's never going to hit there. That was Musial. He was a rare human being, and nobody gave him a hard time about his bat or anything else that had to do with hitting a baseball. However, Mc-Carver, at a tender age, was a different story. Willie Mays would walk past Tim, and in that wonderful high-pitched voice of his would say, "You really gonna go up and hit with that baby bat?" Willie McCovey enjoyed that, and jumped all over it. With his slow Alabama drawl, Stretch would provide the baritone backup for Mays's soprano: "Hey, Tim, you still using that baby bat?" Once, before a game at Candlestick, McCovey picked up one of McCarver's bats, stuck the knob in his mouth, and strolled onto the field using it as a toothpick. To this day, when I call McCarver on the phone, I ask him, "Hey, Tim, you still using that baby bat?"

Not that McCarver was a guy to take lightly. In 1967, he'd finished second to Cepeda in the MVP voting. In addition to his hitting and receiving skills, my buddy played the game with a toughness that I thoroughly appreciated. So did John Roseboro, among others. The Dodgers' catcher was as rough-and-tumble as they came, but there was a memorable moment when McCarver rolled around third base one day and took on Roseboro full-speed. Leo Durocher said it was the hardest home plate collision he'd ever seen. Roseboro was out for a month, but Tim came away from it with only a gashed and bloody face. I told him he'd never looked so good.

Deservedly, McCarver fast became a fan favorite in both St. Louis and back in Memphis, where he opened up a restaurant. Every time he got a hit, they'd ring a bell in the restaurant. And every time he *didn't* get a hit—well, not *every* time, but often enough to leave a lasting impression—he'd stomp on his poor helmet. That went on until 1967, when we got unbreakable helmets, which made him even madder.

In '68, McCarver had fallen off to his worst hitting season since he'd become our regular catcher in 1963. Even so, he'd earned his reputation, was a two-time All-Star, and McLain, showing respect, started him with a curveball.

It caught a lot of the plate, and Tim, in turn, caught a lot of the curveball. He drove it to right-center, between Northrup and Kaline, and the ball reached the fence in two bounces through the shadows. Northrup picked it up cleanly, but McCarver, understanding the depth of the outfield gaps at Busch Memorial, didn't hesitate at second base, looking nothing like a catcher as he sprinted to third and easily beat the relay from Stanley. The throw skipped away from Don Wert at third, but McLain was in place to back it up.

I CAN'T OVERSTATE how badly I wanted that run. Runs were precious anytime in 1968, and more so, it seemed, when I pitched. Of course, I was always pitching against Don Drysdale or Ferguson Jenkins or Bob Veale or Tom Seaver or Juan Marichal or Gaylord Perry—saw every last one of those guys that year, most of them twice. For the life of me, I couldn't comprehend why Red would always match me up that way; but I guess he was no different from the other manager.

At any rate, I always knew we weren't likely to be scoring much, and I was always on edge about it. Flustered, you could say. McCarver would argue with me because I was so eaten up by our inability to score runs that I'd defy the traditional baseball percentages. If we had a lead, for instance, and the bases were loaded, conventional wisdom says that, on a ground ball, your first option is to go for the double play instead of throwing home. Tim would march out and remind me, and I'd say, the hell with that, I'm coming to the plate. I was never willing to give up a run, because I never knew when I might be getting another one.

My first three starts that year, we scored a total of three runs. In Nelson Briles's first three, we scored 25. Good for Nellie; great guy, happy for him. Nevertheless . . . In May, I threw nine shutout innings, gave up a run in the tenth, and lost 1–0 to Woodie Fryman and the Phillies. The next game, I gave up one hit in eight innings and lost 2–0 to Drysdale. After that one, McCarver approached to tell me what a great game I'd pitched, and I lit into him. Said something like, "Great game, my ass. Score some goddamn runs." For the record, I apologized later. What I did, actually, was walk up and whack him, but Tim understood that it was an apology.

The *next* game, I lost 3–1 to Perry, at which point my record was 3–5 with an ERA of 1.52. It got to the point that, when we batted, I was the jackass of the dugout, insulting or cursing or goading the guys in the lineup, trying, if nothing else worked, to shame them into scoring. The pressure was always on; and when we finally put one on the board, it was on even thicker. Flood would say, "Okay, roomie, you got your run. Let's go!"

If I was to get my run this time, in the one-out opportunity we now had in the second inning of game one, it would have to come against the latest and momentarily greatest in the line of Drysdale, Jenkins, Veale, Seaver, Marichal, and Perry—and Jim Lonborg, going back to the previous World Series. This time, the guy on the mound was the 31-game winner himself, the guy who got all the headlines and magazine covers and TV appearances while I was setting the ERA record, the guy with the plane and the Vegas gig, the guy who'd told the world he wanted to demolish us. So, yeah, I hoped like hell to see McCarver trot home from third.

For that to happen, we had the right guy at the plate. Even though he batted sixth in the order, Mike Shannon had led our club with 79 RBIs. That might not sound like a whole lot, and in fact it didn't put him among the top ten in the league—and the league, at that time, consisted of only ten teams—but Shannon had gotten it done for us all year. Besides that, he hit plenty of fly balls, and with McLain working up in the zone as he typically did, I had reason to believe that I'd be heading out for the third inning with an early lead and a little extra pep in my step.

Detroit's infield was positioned in close, to make a play on McCarver if Shannon hit the ball on the ground, but McLain's first pitch was a fastball up and away. That might have seemed like a wrongheaded choice for a pitcher needing to keep the ball out of the outfield, but he was probably thinking strikeout, as I would have in that scenario. No matter how the infield was set up, the breaking ball would be the pitch I'd stay away from if I were trying to avoid a sacrifice fly—it's too easy to hit in the air if not perfectly thrown—and McLain evidently thought the same way. But while he had good reasons for favoring the high fastball, there was also a good reason why it failed him. He was still overthrowing from over the top.

He did it again for ball two, another pitch that, had it found the strike zone, might have missed the bat but might also—and this is the problem a pitcher runs into when he finds himself out of wiggle room—have been just the thing Shannon needed to put us ahead with a run-scoring fly ball or something even better. The Moon Man was strong enough that something better was always a possibility.

He was, in fact, not lacking in tools of any sort, with sufficient talent to switch from right field to third base in 1967 without ever having played the position. I'll admit that, at first, I thought the move was a bad idea, just as I'd questioned the wisdom of swapping Broglio for Brock. Shannon was a good outfielder with an exceptional arm—he'd been a great high school quarterback—but the Cardinals had slipped into a state of transition since trading Ken Boyer after the 1965 season. In return, we got Al Jackson, a very professional left-handed pitcher, and Charley Smith, a traveling third baseman—we were his fifth team in six years—who was asked, perhaps unfairly, to replace Boyer. After a year of that, Smith was turned around for Maris, which left us with two right fielders and a hole at third base. Shannon was game for the experiment.

It was a pleasure, and something of an amusement, to watch him grow into his new position. I wouldn't call him a natural infielder, and it was a while before he was up to speed on the fine points of the hot corner. He once asked me where I wanted him to play certain batters, and I told him not to worry about it because the ball wouldn't be hit to him unless there was a runner on first base with less than two outs and a right-handed hitter at the plate, in which case all he'd have to do is pick up the ball and throw it to second base to start the double play. When it soon happened just like that, to end an inning, Mike strode directly over to me in the dugout, all pumped up, and asked me how I knew the ball would be coming right to him. It was because that situation was one of the few times when I would throw a two-seamer on the plate, down and in; but of course that's not what I told Shannon. I just told him I was smart, that's how.

At any rate, his willingness and abilities made him popular with his teammates—we were also entertained by his unique, cosmic views on just about everything—and St. Louis. Shannon was a homegrown guy from the south side of town, the son of a police officer who became the city's prosecuting attorney, and as a prep star at Christian Brothers College High School, where one of his teammates was Stan Musial's son, Dick, he had been the Missouri Player of the Year in both football and basketball. Generally speaking, Mike was to St. Louis what McCarver (who, ironically, also made his name at a high school called Christian Brothers) was to Memphis. I wish I could extend that parallel to me and Omaha, but—although the city did have a day for me after the '67 Series—it doesn't really hold up, in part because, when I'd started high school, the coach declared me too puny for football. McCarver, on the other hand, had football offers from Notre Dame and Tennessee. For his part, Shannon earned a scholarship to the University of Missouri, and there were some who thought that, if he'd stayed there instead of signing with the Cardinals, he would have become a serious Heisman Trophy candidate. Much as basketball was my best sport as a kid, football was Shannon's.

But he was good enough at baseball to finish seventh in the MVP voting for 1968, and plenty good enough to get hold of one of those high fastballs from McLain. At 2-and-0, though, McLain turned again to the sidearm option that was getting him strikes. This time, the pitch angled over the inner half of the plate and Shannon pounced on it, smashing it past third base, foul by inches.

The at-bat was now resembling Cepeda's, with McLain falling behind in the count before rallying back by lowering his release point. With two balls, a strike, and a lot to consider, he went into his four-corners routine, then glanced at McCarver on third, wound up, and placed a crisp overhand fastball on the outside edge, where Shannon reached to poke it foul.

That drew McLain into position to close out the battle with a sidearm finishing pitch, as he had Cepeda. First, though, he requested a new ball from Gorman and walked it to the back of the mound. When he returned, in no hurry, to the rubber, he shook off Freehan and let loose with a sidearm fastball, high and away, headed for ball three, except that Shannon swung under it for the second out.

———

AT THIS POINT, I wished McLain were left-handed. If that had been the case, I'd have liked our chances with Julian Javier up next, no matter how many outs there were.

For the season, Javier had batted .368 against lefties and only .206 against right-handers, with more power, more patience, more everything against the former. It had been that way, as a rule, his whole career. And yet, in spite of his difficulty hitting right-handers, Javier, in 1968, had made his second All-Star team. He was that good at virtually everything else.

In the minor leagues, he'd been regarded as maybe the fastest prospect in the game. From the time he came to the Cardinals in 1960—a May trade with the Pirates for veteran pitcher Vinegar Bend Mizell, which the club announced by presenting the starting lineup that night—until Brock arrived in 1964, he led the team in stolen bases every year. He had enough power to surprise you now and again. He was a terrific bunter. And defensively, he was magnificent. I thought he was a better second baseman than Bill Mazeroski, who was elected to the Hall of Fame on his defense. In my estimation, Javier was the best around at as many as four things a second baseman has to do: charge a weakly hit ground ball; range to his right, control his body, and make the tough throw to first; sprint into the outfield for over-the-shoulder catches of pop flies; and turn the double play. His ability to elude a base runner as he received a throw, pivoted, and relayed it to first was so uncanny that we called him the Phantom. It was like he vanished the instant the ball left his hand.

He was also sharply tuned into the game. Hoolie knew, for instance, that Flood, as great as he was with the glove, had a weak throwing arm and tended to play a deep center field. So when Flood made a play with runners on base, Javier would sprint out an extra fifty feet or more to take the relay. That was the sort of heads-up, team-centered baseball that made the Cardinals special, and that made Javier a great fit for our ball club, in spite of the fact that he was our only Spanish speaker until Cepeda showed up.

Since the Pirates had Mazeroski, Javier had not played in the big leagues before the trade, at which point he was immediately installed in our starting lineup. He was only the third major leaguer from the Dominican Republic, following Ozzie Virgil and Felipe Alou. Later in 1960, they were joined by four others, including Marichal and Matty Alou. Those were the Dominican trailblazers, and Javier, for one, took that role to heart. He later founded and owned several teams in the D.R. Among the island players he inspired was his son, Stan, named after Musial.

As Javier stepped to the plate and adjusted his glasses in the second inning, with two outs, McCarver still on third, and a history-making right-hander squinting in for the sign, he did have this going for him: in his last World Series appearance, game seven of '67, facing Lonborg—Boston's *right-handed* ace— he'd belted a sixth-inning, three-run homer to effectively knock out the Red Sox. On the flip side, what typically made him miserable was any pitch a right-hander threw off-speed, crooked, or sidearm.

Sidearm was what he got, first thing. A fastball, low and away. Javier was pleased to let it pass.

When an overhand fastball stayed high and outside, McLain was behind 2-and-0 for the second time in the inning. He'd been pitching at a recurring disadvantage that he'd so far been able to overcome. Twice when he'd been behind Cepeda, and once when he'd been behind Shannon, he'd chosen to drop down to catch up. I hoped that Javier remembered that. If he'd wandered by the dugout, I'd have reminded him.

I tended to track opposing pitchers in that way, watching for tipoffs and patterns. For example, there had been a game in 1966 when I locked up with Bob Veale in one of those 1–0 affairs. Veale was a big left-hander who featured a fastball in the upper 90s, but he also liked to throw his slider. On this night, he was having trouble finding the strike zone with his fastball and kept falling behind 2-and-0. Just like McLain was doing. Then he'd turn to his slider—just like McLain was doing with his sidearm stuff—and break a bat. I was perturbed, as usual, about our inability to score, and in the dugout I'd been ragging our hitters: "You guys are stupid. Don't you see what he's doing? Fastball, fastball, slider. Come on!" When I stepped to the plate one time, sure enough, Veale threw the fastball, ball one, and then another fastball, ball two, and now I knew the slider was coming. I smacked it over Matty Alou's head in center field and cruised in with a double. Naturally, when I got to second base I made a show of looking into our dugout, just to bask for a moment in my triumph and superior intelligence—rub it in a little, you know—and the place was *empty*. They'd all gone and hid. They didn't want to hear about it. While my cohorts were making themselves scarce, I went ahead and stole third. And was stranded there, of course.

So anyway, McLain, sticking to the sequence, went sidearm on 2-and-0. The ball clipped the outside corner, around the upper edge of the zone. Gorman called it a strike. Javier turned and looked at him, then stepped out of the box, scooped up some dirt, rubbed his hands together—no batting glove—and spat on them.

At 2-and-1, the count on which McLain had shown Shannon an overhand fastball, he did the same to Javier. This one, though, flashed above the letters. Javier was mightily tempted to swing at it and actually started to, then stopped and swiveled, a twenty-first-century strike but ball three in 1968.

All right, 3-1, hitter's count. Come on, Hoolie.

Sidearm fastball. Fouled back. Full count.

And now a sidearm *curve*—the pitch he'd gotten Cepeda with—on the hands, over the plate. Javier froze. Gorman's arm went up. McCarver trotted in to get his gear on.

Damn.

If nothing else, though, we now had a line on Denny McLain.

	1	2	3	4	5	6	7	8	9	R	H	E
Tigers	0	0								0	1	0
Cardinals	0	0								0	1	0

(CREDIT: *THE SPORTING NEWS*/GETTY IMAGES)

Brock was always at his best in the World Series. In 1967, when he demolished the Red Sox and set a record with seven stolen bases, I thought he should have won the Series MVP award instead of the guy on his left here. He would go on to tie that record against the Tigers.

Third Inning

MCLAIN HAD GIVEN me an idea. For the first pitch to Bill Freehan, leading off the third, McCarver called for a slider and I gave it to him sidearm. But I had strayed from my natural habitat; it stayed flat and missed outside. Enough of that. The slider that followed came from my regular three-quarters slot, started off in the same direction, broke down and out—a '68 special—and Freehan hacked at it for strike one. We were back to business as usual.

By at least one standard, Freehan had been the best everyday player in the American League that year. With 25 home runs and his fourth straight Gold Glove—he also led the AL for the second year in a row at being hit by pitches, with an impressive twenty-four, the most in fifty-seven years (although, at the same time, Ron Hunt, a St. Louis native, was hit twenty-*five* times in the National League, none of which, I might add, involved me, in spite of the fact that Hunt walked into six of my more strategic fastballs over the course of his painful career)—he'd finished second to McLain in the MVP voting.

Those two, in spite of working so well together as a battery, were an unlikely pairing. While McLain felt no obligation to appear in the Tigers' dugout if he wasn't pitching, Freehan represented its heart. As a former Wolverine, his rah-rah spirit was so collegiate that his teammates called him Big Ten. To McLain, that kind of stuff was for chumps. He had little use, also, for other things that Freehan observed devoutly, such as punctuality, accountability, and the traditions of the game. Freehan bristled at some of the stunts McLain pulled, like stopping over in Las Vegas, coming and going—never bothering with bed, either time—when Freehan hitched a ride on McLain's private jet to the 1968 All-Star Game in Houston. On another occasion, McLain flew his plane to a game he was pitching in Cleveland, put down halfway for an emergency landing, arrived about thirty minutes before the national anthem, brought mediocre stuff to the mound, and threw a shutout, as Freehan figured he would. The two of them, to me, were a case in point that teammates don't have to be all lovey-dovey to prosper together on the field. They regularly argued over pitching approach and the responsibilities of a big-league ballplayer. It offended Freehan that McLain could make so much success look so easy. And yet, Freehan was quick to acknowledge that he'd never caught a better pitcher. He said he'd love to have four McLains in the Detroit rotation.

Of course, none of that mattered to me in the top of the third, as Freehan planted his six-foot-three-inch, footballish frame a few inches from the perimeter of the plate. It was easy to see why he was plunked so often, and why American Leaguers pitched him tight in the first place. I'd pick my spots in that regard, and this wasn't one of them. I had no interest in putting the leadoff batter on base, gratuitously.

So I stuck a fastball on the outside corner, and while Freehan let it pass, Gorman honored it as strike two.

I was less satisfied with the ump's next call, however. It was a fastball that I thought caught the outside edge at the top of the strike zone. Freehan went after it, his hands sweeping across his body, the end of his bat extending toward Javier and his right elbow—the second arm through—pointing all the way to Shannon. The bat decisively crossed the plate, but the knob stayed in front of the head, which meant that Freehan hadn't broken his wrists. That was the standard which umpires tended to use at the time to characterize a swing. And so, instead of putting one out in the book, I still had work to do—a *lot* of work, as it turned out—against a guy who'd hit as many home runs as the Tigers' cleanup batter, tied for fifth in the league.

I returned to the slider, in that favored spot of mine on—or maybe just off—the outside corner at the knees. Freehan got a sliver of it.

My next slider wasn't nearly as good. Sometimes, though, it's better to miss badly than barely. This one, high and round—I got under it—was awful enough to not even interest Freehan. Three-and-two.

When a batter hangs around that long, he improves his chances of seeing a mistake pitch. In a typical game, I served up maybe twenty or twenty-five of those. On a few of them, I'd just get lucky, the percentages would cut me some slack, and the batter would fail to take advantage. On a few, the pitch would be so fat and out of context that it would throw the guy off. A few might be hit hard, but right at Maxvill or Flood or somebody. And a few, inevitably, would burn me. The more you kept the hitters off balance with good stuff, good selection, and good, variable locations, the fewer times that would happen. But there would be no multiple choices if you made a mistake to somebody like Willie Mays; although, when it came to hitting mistake pitches, there was really nobody else like him. Willie Mays did not hit singles off hanging breaking balls.

In 1968, my control was sharp enough that I made fewer mistakes than ever before; or ever after, for that matter. But I made some, and I made one on the seventh pitch to Bill Freehan. I might have been a little out of sorts from the previous pitch, when I'd overthrown and lost my rhythm and screwed up the release. Maybe, after that, I overcompensated. Whatever the reason, I now presented a fastball at the belt, in the middle of the plate, to a powerful hitter who knew what to do with such a pitch.

He fouled it straight back. Glory be.

I knew I was now, officially, fortunate, and I also knew I shouldn't push my luck. It was time to do something a little different. With a full count, I needn't fret anymore over putting Freehan on base with a ball to the body. *Any* ball would put him on base. That meant the inside corner was in play. What's more, looming over the plate like he did, he was making the strike zone appear smaller, which I couldn't tolerate.

I brought the fastball in on him. Once again, Freehan fouled it back.

At this point, the checked-swing call had cost me four extra pitches, with the fifth to come. Although I wasn't counting at the time—I never counted or cared—I'd thrown 17 pitches in the first inning and 11 in the second. Those weren't problematic numbers, but muggy days and the World Series both take their tolls. With twenty-one outs still to get, I was ready for Freehan to go away.

Ordinarily, I would not, repeat *not*, throw a slow breaking pitch to a big guy on 3-and-2 with nobody out. But I was having a good curveball day, and he hadn't seen one, and he was being difficult. So I pulled down on the baseball as I let it go and it broke nicely from the inner half to the outer half. Freehan was well in front of it, reaching. He rapped it past third base, foul.

When I shook off McCarver before the tenth pitch, I did it with a twitch of my glove against my thigh. I'd like to tell you that, when I twitched my glove against my thigh, it was a particular, coded kind of shake-off, one that meant I liked the pitch but not the location or liked the pitch and intended to throw it but was shaking it off just to mess with the batter. I did that sometimes, with my glove or head, either one. Sometimes Tim would actually give me a sign to do it. But this was a no-fake shake-off, and I really don't know why I twitched my glove instead of my head. Just felt like it, I guess. And I wanted to throw my slider again.

It was a '68 special, and it may or may not have clipped the corner when it crossed Freehan's knees. And he may or may not have gone around just a tiny bit farther than he had on the fourth pitch. I believe it did and he did. More important, Gorman believed one or the other; I'm not sure which and don't care. For his part, Frechan felt that it didn't and he didn't. He took a couple steps toward Gorman and said so before trudging back to the third-base dugout.

These days, in spite of the outcome, the announcer would declare that a great at-bat. Maybe so. It was long and stubborn. Freehan competed hard, and I lost some water weight. But when I turned to get the ball from Shannon, after we'd thrown it around the infield, there was one out and nobody on, with the eight- and nine-hole batters coming up.

DON WERT WAS not the typical Tiger. He was small and quiet—they called him Coyote because of the high-pitched yipping he produced when asked to talk it up on the infield—and better with the glove than the bat, which is why he was stashed at eighth in Detroit's loaded order, a spot where third basemen are not customarily found.

Defensively, Wert was considered second-best in the American League at his position—to Brooks Robinson, naturally—and good enough to make the 1968 All-Star team in spite of batting only .200. His All-Star pinch-hit appearance, in which he doubled off Tom Seaver, came only a couple weeks after the beaning he suffered in Cleveland, which shattered Wert's helmet and put him in the hospital for a couple nights. He was hitting .224 at the time. When he returned to the lineup, he came to bat wearing a helmet with an earflap.

Wert had been raised in the Dutch Country of Lancaster County, Pennsylvania, where he was loading hundred-pound feed sacks for the local Farm Bureau when the Tigers signed him. In the subsequent off-seasons, he headed home and sold sporting goods at Sears, Roebuck, even after taking over as the Tigers' regular third baseman in 1964. The following year, he played in every game; and although he never hit a whole lot, he went on to hold his full-time job for seven years. For most of those, Wert was overshadowed by the likes of Kaline, Cash, Horton, Freehan, Northrup, and McAuliffe; but on September 17, 1968, he secured his place in Tiger history, singling to right field in the ninth to bring home Kaline with the run that beat the Yankees and clinched the American League pennant.

I didn't know it as he took his place in the batter's box, and it wouldn't have mattered if I had, but a strikeout of Wert would be my sixth in a row and tie a World Series record. I had my breaking stuff to thank for the previous five, and started Wert with a slider. His swing came up empty as the ball dipped over the outside corner.

When he stood at the plate, his earflap facing me and his other ear in front of Tom Gorman, Wert came up only to the umpire's shoulder. He made himself even shorter when he leveraged his swing with a hard rotation that drove his right knee toward the ground, as he did when I threw him a low fastball on the second pitch. He fouled it back, in the air. That was happening a lot.

Wert had been slightly behind the fastball, and with two strikes I reasoned that he'd focus on quickening his stroke. So I threw him a slider that he didn't go for, either because he was geared for another fastball, as I'd expected, or because he knew, somehow, that Gorman would say it missed the outside corner.

The pitch looked good enough, at least, that it was worth another shot. I don't second-guess the rationale; but with a count of 1-and-2, there was no excuse for hanging the next one the way I did, waist-high and centered. It was the kind of slider that Willie Mays would not hit for a single. Wert, however, did, cracking it sharply into center field as his right knee thumped in the dirt.

Now, damn it, McLain could bunt.

McLAIN WAS A hell of a bunter. I thought *I* was a good bunter, and I had seven sacrifices in '68. McLain led the American League with *sixteen*—twice as many as my best year. And this was a guy known to blow off batting practice. He had an extraordinary feel for playing the game.

That feel for the game, I believe—the aptitude and talent for doing what had to be done—was the overriding reason he was able to win 31 times. By other measures, McLain was not the best pitcher in his league, even in 1968. Five AL pitchers put together earned run averages under 2.00, with his ranking fourth, well behind the leader, Luis Tiant of Cleveland (Sam McDowell was second at 1.81, Dave McNally third at 1.95, and Tommy John fifth at 1.98), whose 1.60 was built by permitting, to that point, the fewest hits per nine innings in major-league history. Even with that historic feat, Tiant won ten fewer games than McLain.

Overall, the pitching was even more dominant that year in the American League than the National. That's in spite of my record ERA (which was followed by Bob Bolin's 1.99, Bob Veale's 2.05, Jerry Koosman's 2.08, Steve Blass's 2.12, Don Drysdale's 2.15, and Tom Seaver's 2.20), Drysdale's streak of consecutive scoreless innings—six straight shutouts and change—and Marichal's 26–9 record with 30 complete games. In the American League, only Yastrzemski batted over .300, and only by a point. The National League, while keeping the covers on the balls, at least had five guys in the .300s, including Pete Rose at .335 and two Alous (Matty and Felipe).

As a league, the NL hit .243 and the AL but .230. The National League's cumulative ERA was 2.99, the American's 2.98. But that's splitting hairs. The fact is, big-league hitters, loop to loop and coast to coast, were historically overmatched in 1968. When the best of them came together for the All-Star Game, the only run scored was *unearned*, on a double-play grounder from McCovey. It got so bad for the Pittsburgh Pirates that they dragged fifty bats to the bullpen and burned them. Speaking for the Pirates' pitching staff, Elroy Face, their great reliever, said that if the club went one more game without scoring, they'd start burning the *hitters*.

The response from the game itself was to burn the top third of the mound, more or less. After the season, the summit from which we ruled was reduced from a height of fifteen inches to ten, which of course lowered the angle at which the ball slanted toward home plate. I'd have preferred to remain as high and mighty as possible, but I'm unconvinced about the effect that had; although curveball pitchers would probably tell you something different. The way my curve was hooking and falling on October second, I suppose I should show some respect for the extra altitude.

For me, though, the bigger modification came in the strike zone, which I've never really had a clear understanding of anyway. In '68, the top of it was around the batter's armpit. In '69, it was somewhere below that, ostensibly at the letters. There was also some sneaky little squeezing at the knees and corners. To this day, the definition of a strike remains fluid and vague to me. Depends on the year. And the umpire. And sometimes the *inning.*

The changes inspired by 1968—which, less officially but I suspect no less significantly, also included more warnings to pitchers on pitches that drifted inside—have since been referred to as the Gibson Rules. I can assure you I was not consulted. Nor was I flattered, much preferring not to be associated, in any fashion, with legislation that would diminish the power of the pitcher. The actions taken by Major League Baseball were not only sudden—the sixties, to a great extent, had been characterized by Hall of Fame hitting from the likes of Mays, Aaron, McCovey, Clemente, Yastrzemski, Mantle, Kaline, Cepeda, Frank Robinson, Harmon Killebrew, Ernie Banks, and Billy Williams; the existing regulations didn't present much of a problem for those guys in 1961 or 1966—but monumental. The lowering of the mound represented the first time since the end of the dead-ball era, nearly half a century prior, that the actual properties of the game had been altered. I disavow responsibility. As far as that goes, McLain, after all, was the one who generated most of the buzz. If we have to pin the flattening of the mound and the shrinking of the strike zone on some complicit pitcher, I suggest we call them the McLain Rules. Denny might even like the irony of that, given how he felt about rules in general.

He certainly wouldn't have minded a lower strike zone when he came up to bunt in the third inning. I wasn't an easy guy to bunt against, because high fastballs are tough to get to the ground and I specialized in those. McLain saw one, right off, and bunted it to the screen.

He bunted the second fastball—not as high as the first—over the near corner of our dugout, in the vicinity of McLain's idol, Frank Sinatra.

Maybe he was distracted. He bunted the third one in between the other two. Three of those is all you get.

As fine a year as I'd had, and in spite of leading the National League in strikeouts, there hadn't been a game in which I'd fanned seven batters the first time through the order; hadn't been a game quite like *this* one. So far.

THE FIRST OF those strikeouts had been McAuliffe, on a couple four-seamers at the belly. I was in no hurry to add another one, since strikeouts cost pitches and I'd already spent ten on Freehan. I was in a bigger hurry to get back to the dugout.

If I could've had my druthers, I'd have taken a first-pitch ground ball to Maxvill or Javier. But, as always, there were extenuating circumstances. One: the pitch for that would be a two-seamer, which McAuliffe was likely to top and pull and maybe smack in the direction of first base, where Cepeda was holding

Wert and then squaring in front of the bag, limiting his range and reaction time; opening up a hitting hole, in other words. And two: McAuliffe had seen enough fastballs in his first at-bat, and had taken good enough swings at them, that he was probably up there just waiting to whale at the next one.

On the other hand, when he'd led off the game, I had no idea my curveball would be humoring me the way it was. At that point, it was an afterthought. Two innings later, it had become a compelling alternative; a go-to pitch.

So I went to it, and it indulged me once more, swerving handsomely onto the outside corner for called strike one.

That changed the working dynamic. I'd screwed with McAuliffe's timing a bit, maybe muddied the expectations he'd brought to the plate. Given him pause. Tempered his aggressiveness. Now I could throw the fastball down.

I really didn't mean to throw it *in*, though, the way I did, and I definitely didn't mean for McAuliffe to crack it sharply toward Cepeda. But Cha Cha was shifted and ready, the ball found him in the cut of the grass on one agreeable hop, and I didn't even have to cover first base.

After Freehan, the next three Tigers had consumed only nine pitches. All right.

Now for some damn runs.

I LOVED HAVING Dal Maxvill behind me on the infield. I didn't feel the same way about having him ahead of me in the lineup.

Maxie earned a Gold Glove in 1968, and probably should have won more of them. He made all the plays at shortstop, was a great complement to Javier, saved me some runs, and worked hard at his craft. At 150-something pounds—Bob Broeg of the *Post-Dispatch* called him "the Thin Man"—he was never going to do a lot of damage as a hitter and accepted it, concentrating his energies on the defensive talent that fed his family. That part of it, I couldn't understand. Dal and I were on the same page about a lot of things—our mutual appreciation for a good glass of wine with a good dinner and good conversation on the road, for instance—but his attitude toward hitting was something I simply wasn't able to accept. It seemed to me that a proud professional ballplayer with a .217 lifetime average would take a little extra batting practice now and then. Not Maxvill. When I asked him about it—*challenged* him about it, you might say— he told me, "I didn't get here by hitting." Hmm.

Maxvill had grown up across the river in Granite City, Illinois, a fan of the Cardinals and son of a steelworker. His mother actually managed his first Khoury League team, hauling the equipment around on a bicycle and carrying little Dal on the handlebars, something I'd like to have seen. He later turned down some baseball scholarships and attended Washington University in St. Louis for engineering, ultimately signing with the Cardinals after a tryout. They were looking for defense.

He nearly quit in the minor leagues to go home and sell fuses, joined us in 1962, started all seven games of the 1964 World Series at second base when Javier was injured, became our everyday shortstop in 1966, sold fuses in the winter, knocked a triple off the center-field wall against Jim Lonborg to get us going in game seven of the '67 Series, and followed that up in '68 with a career-high average of .253. In seven more major-league seasons, Maxvill would never again exceed .225. In 1970, he set National League records for the fewest hits and total bases by a batter who played in at least 150 games.

Maxie did walk a fair amount, and in '68 led the team in that category. That made no sense to me, because I couldn't imagine why a pitcher wouldn't just pour the ball over the plate against him. This was a guy who hit fewer home runs than yours truly, by a long shot. Six in fourteen years. When fortune hands you a hitter like that, you *cannot* put him on base. But some pitchers, including some very good ones, had a tendency to lose focus against players they perceived as easy outs.

McLain fell into that category. It was one of the things about him that confounded Bill Freehan.

The first pitch was high and tight, and Maxvill, choked up on the bat, checked his swing. Ball one.

The second was outside.

The third was up and in again.

At 3-and-0, McLain turned around, pawed at the dirt with his spikes, pushed up the short right sleeve of his undershirt, stepped up to the rubber, threw an uncontested fastball a couple inches under Maxie's knee, and dropped his arms in disgust.

IT WAS ONE thing to squander McCarver's triple. But to waste a leadoff walk to Maxvill would be an offense to the base-ball gods—and not just because it was Maxvill. It was *McLain*. The best pitcher in the American League was off his game, and we needed to hold him accountable. We needed to score *now*.

Which meant that I needed to get a bunt down.

I didn't at all mind bunting, and I especially didn't mind bunt-ing in a situation like this; but I did enjoy taking my cuts when I could. I'd won a conference batting title at Creighton, and I don't think there was ever a point in my pitching career when part of me didn't wish I was playing center field on a daily basis.

When the Cardinals signed me, they weren't sure whether I'd pitch or shag flies. I was open, also, to the possibility of third base or even catching, which were both on my résumé. Johnny Keane was the manager of the Omaha team I reported to, and just to get an idea of what he had on his hands he asked me, first thing, to throw some pitches to the Omaha batters. When none of them managed to hit a fair ball—in large part due to my wildness—my career as an outfielder was over. I still believe I could have been a pretty good one, if not Curt Flood.

That said, I had the same trouble hitting in 1968 as everybody else. More than most, in fact. Maxie outhit me. I even thought about going up to the plate left-handed, just to change the karma. I'd been a switch-hitter through college, and I always took some left-handed hacks in batting practice, but I didn't want to expose my right arm to an errant or unfriendly fastball and the Cardinals didn't want me to, either. Schoendienst accused me of not having the guts to bat left-handed anyway, which I considered a challenge, so once, in 1967, I stepped into the other box when Ferguson Jenkins was pitching. I hit Fergie in the belly with a line drive. He threw me out, but I felt pretty good about it. Not good enough, though, to actually try it again, even while batting .170 in '68. The best thing I did at the plate that year was bunt.

So I would not be a happy camper if I failed to move Maxvill over to second base. Before that could happen, though, I had to wait as Freehan walked out to talk to McLain—to deliver a bunt-defense plan or a take-a-deep-breath-and-just-throw-strikes message or both—and then McLain called him back for a moment. Of course, none of that made any difference to me. I'd be getting high fastballs from McLain, just as McLain got them in the top of the inning.

If the first one or two came in a little too high to put on the ground, I wouldn't hesitate to wait for a better candidate. If necessary, I was pretty sure I could get a bunt down with a strike or two, besides which, if McLain were inclined to keep walking the bottom of the order, I was inclined to give him full cooperation.

His first pitch arrived from the sidearm slot, up in the zone and tailing toward me. I pulled the bat back and Gorman signaled strike one.

So much for the base on balls.

The next one was also on the inner half, but more buntable, and I dropped it on the grass in front and to the left of McLain. He picked it up easily, threw to McAuliffe, covering first, and Maxvill scooted along to scoring position, from where Flood would surely drive him in if Brock, my money man, was unable to.

THERE WERE SOME similarities, it seemed to me, between McLain and Juan Marichal; and not just because they were the league leaders in wins for 1968. They both threw over the top, primarily, but sometimes changed their arm angle. McLain didn't have Marichal's big, chorus-line leg kick, but then hardly anybody did. They were both durable and instinctive and right-handed, with good but not overwhelming velocity and a broad command of the art of pitching. Of course, maybe all that was just wishful thinking on my part. Because Brock could hit Marichal.

At least, there was a time when he could. It lasted until they met up once at an airport and Marichal—I'm telling you, the guy was crafty—commenced to sweet-talk Lou about how great a hitter he was. "Lou Brock . . . You always hit very well against me." Brock was flattered, of course, and sweet-talked Marichal right back. "No, Juan, I always have trouble with you," he said.

"You got a damn good screwball . . ." Well, after that, Marichal gave him nothing but screwballs, and the party was over.

McLain might have been a bit of a screwball himself, but he didn't *throw* one, as far as I knew. So I was hopeful. I could envision a smash down the third-base line, past Don Wert, who was playing in-close to defend against a bunt, and then Lou racing around to second base, at least, and very possibly third, which would be just like him, because he was not only a prime-time hitter but had gotten a lot of mileage out of smashing the ball down the third-base line or maybe wide of it, either way shooting it past the drawn-in third baseman, which was a hell of a skill for a left-handed hitter. It was ironic that third basemen would invariably play him that way, since Lou hardly ever bunted, unless Sandy Koufax was pitching; and that ended one day in 1965 when Koufax, who didn't like to be bunted on and later admitted it was the only time he ever threw at a batter, broke Lou's shoulder. Lou only missed five games from that, although, when he returned to the lineup, the shoulder clearly wasn't right because he started 0-for-20. But he wouldn't sit out an inning more than he had to, because he was as tough as they came. Regardless of the beating he took from pitchers, or from running the bases as hard as he did, you almost never saw Brock in the training room.

Anyway, if Koufax wasn't pitching, the third baseman really had no business crowding my friend like that. Of course, it was quite all right with Lou and the rest of us, because, like I said before, he was the most opportunistic of ballplayers.

In one sense, Brock's hitting was overshadowed by his speed, and in another, his hitting was *set up* by his speed. At any rate, the man had more than 3,000 hits in the major leagues. Except for not bunting enough—to this day, when I see Lou, I'm hoping he drops one down—he learned how to take advantage of the adjustments the pitchers and fielders made against him. He also adjusted very well to spotlights and circumstances. He batted nearly .400 over twenty-one World Series games.

And so, as McLain checked Maxvill at second and let loose with a fastball, away—the very pitch Brock could powder between Wert's hat and head, as the little third baseman ducked it between his shoulders—I was *very* hopeful.

Foul back.

Apparently, there was movement or some kind of deception to McLain's fastball that we couldn't see from the dugout and doesn't show up on the low-grade video. Or maybe the trouble was Lou's bat. He tossed it aside and took another one from the batboy.

He neglected to swing it, however, when the following fastball came in belt-high and barely off the inside corner. It pains me, even now, even on low-grade video, to watch that pitch go by, unpunished. Gotta hit that, Lou!

Instead, he tapped the next one, on a bounce, to McLain's left. Maxvill took off for third as the contact was made. When McLain whirled around, Maxie was only halfway there, beyond Stanley and out of options. McLain was a good baseball player who knew exactly what to do, which was run at the runner. Maxie elected to scramble back toward second, but McLain, on the move, tossed the ball on the mark to Stanley, who got to the bag before Dal did—McAuliffe was there, too, for that matter—and tagged him on the foot.

But hey, Brock was on first. For him, that was scoring position.

———

THE TIGERS PITCHED out. Lou didn't go. Advantage, Brock.

I thought McLain actually balked on the pitch. He changed his rhythm, sped up his stretch motion, and hurried through his stop. He also stepped off, threw to first, landscaped; and was generally distracted. That was the Brock effect. Pitchers hated the havoc he brought down on them. They hated even more when he stole bases when we were ahead by four or five runs, which frankly wasn't often. But it happened, and Lou had no conscience about taking a base that was there to be taken. I admired him for that. He was a competitor after my own heart. Lou was out there to beat the other team, and whatever the situation or score, he went about that business with everything he had.

There were, however, repercussions. Lou was thrown at a lot. Lonborg had made him duck in the '67 Series. Al McBean of the Pirates hit him in the head. And when things like that happened, it was my obligation to answer. The responsibility of protecting Brock played a large part in the reputation that still follows me around. But I was being a teammate, not a thug; and if the act of retaliation got me misunderstood, so be it. As a pitcher, I didn't *want* to be understood. I wanted an edge, not a comfort level. In an opponent, I much preferred fear to friendship. So, no, I didn't resent what I had to do for Lou. I only resented when a teammate *asked* me to knock somebody down. They didn't have to ask. Brock never did.

Usually, when Lou provoked the other side, everybody knew the drill, anyway. Like the game against Cincinnati in 1967—two starts before Clemente broke my leg—when we pounded Milt Pappas right out of the gate, starting with a double from Brock, and by the time Lou batted for the second time in the first inning it was 7–0, one out, and Don Nottebart had taken over for Pappas. I had singled ahead of Lou, and his ground ball forced me at second. But that left him on first, and since the Reds still had eight innings to catch up, he went ahead and made for second. He was thrown out, but that didn't appease Cincinnati. When Lou batted again in the fourth inning, Nottebart nailed him.

As a result, I naturally threw a fastball rather close to Tony Perez leading off the fifth. Tony eventually flied out to Maris, but on his way to the dugout he had a few accented words for me as he passed the mound. I, in turn, had a few Omaha words for him, which brought Cepeda to the scene to separate us. With that, a big Reds relief pitcher, Bob "Moose" Lee, came charging in from the bullpen. By the time he arrived, there was quite a crowd, and Lee pushed his way through it, yelling "Where's Cepeda? Where's Cepeda?" Being the obliging sort of fellow that he was, Orlando approached Lee from behind, tapped him on the shoulder, and, when Moose turned around, put him down with one punch. That set off the best baseball fight I've ever participated in. I somehow ended up in the Reds' dugout duking it out with Perez, Pete Rose, and Tommy Helms. Our little ruckus lasted until I saw one of my teammates, Bobby Tolan, at the top of the dugout, poised to leap into the pile. I shouted something like, "Look out, that fool's gonna jump us!" We all scattered, and Tolan landed headfirst on the bench. Bob Bauman, our trainer, refused to treat him on the basis of stupidity. The more serious casualty was the policeman who came out of it with a dislocated jaw. I was a little banged-up, like a lot of others, but stayed in the game and managed to last into the eighth inning, with a dozen strikeouts and not a single hit batter.

Most of that episode was on Lou, and while I thought that, in general, he could have been a little more sensitive to the consequences of his style, he did liven things up over a long season. He kept our juices flowing. He was also the best thing about our offense. I only wished he wouldn't complain to the umpires so much. Johnny Bench once told me that Brock did more bickering than any other batter in the league. I don't know if any umpires actually took it out on me, but I'd rather not have been at risk in that way. I needed my corners.

After the pitchout from McLain, everybody in the ballpark knew Lou would be running now, and tens of thousands raised their voices to nudge him along. McLain responded with a virtual pitchout—high and wide—if not an actual one, but Brock, as usual, got a great jump and Freehan's throw was late and off-target, to McAuliffe's left. The ball continued into center field and after sliding a little awkwardly Lou continued on to third, where, asking for time, he took a few moments to walk around, bend over, and jiggle his right shoulder. Bauman paid him a visit, but when he left the field, Brock, as usual, didn't.

Flood, who was a patient man, was accustomed to waiting for one thing or another when Lou was on base. On this occasion he used the time to do a little thinking, then stepped readily into the box, stepped out again, and rubbed his right eye. He may have had something in it, and he may have been pretending that he did as he checked where Wert was positioned. Unlike Brock, Flood was an effective and frequent drag-bunter, and if he could lay down a good one here it would, in all likelihood, bring Lou home from third.

To that end, he could be pretty certain of a strike from McLain, who on cue delivered one sidearm. It was on the outer half of the plate, and Flood, in motion, shortened up and guided the ball in the direction of third base. Brock would have scored easily if it had stayed fair, although I was surprised how quickly McLain got over to pick it up a couple feet over the line. The man was impressive.

Brock, meanwhile, was still on his mind as McLain again drifted to the rubber, faced the plate, and leaned lightly on his right leg, his right shoulder slightly dipped, his hands together, ball and glove held just above his belt. He was not so concerned with Brock that he resorted to the stretch position, but before winding up, while the world's greatest base stealer took his walking leadoff, he backed away to reboot. Then he stepped up and quick-pitched.

An overhand fastball, outside corner. A swing and miss for the second strike.

There was gamesmanship in McLain. Now he stood in front of the mound, looking at Brock as Lou, looking back from third base, discreetly shook his right arm. Then, still changing speeds in his work pace—more so, perhaps, than his pitches—my worthy opponent moved quickly to the rubber, got his sign, glanced again at Brock, wound briskly, and brought the overhand fastball.

High. Full count.

As Freehan put down his signals for the 3-2 pitch, I wondered if, in addition to the basic call and maybe the location, they indicated McLain's arm slot, overhand or sidearm. Doubted it. McLain controlled his game in as many ways as he could think of.

For the fifth time in Flood's two at-bats, he turned to the sidearm: a fastball, high and tight and in the zone. For whatever reason—I credit the full package that McLain presented to him and kept him off balance with—Curt couldn't inside-out this one. He popped it behind the mound, where Stanley called off Wert and put it away.

Forty-seven years, and we *still* haven't gotten that run in.

	1	2	3	4	5	6	7	8	9	R	H	E
Tigers	0	0	0							0	2	1
Cardinals	0	0	0							0	1	0

(Copyright Bettmann/Corbis/AP Images)

Nobody has won thirty games in a season since Denny McLain did it
in 1968. No other pitcher has drunk as many Pepsi-Colas, broken as
many team rules, or played the organ as famously as McLain did. And
there has never been another World Series game in which both starting
pitchers had won the Cy Young and Most Valuable Player awards that
year.

Fourth Inning

THE FIRST TIME around, Mickey Stanley had singled on a slider. But it wasn't a *good* slider—certainly not one that I intended or expected to duplicate—and it didn't dissuade me from giving him another. If anything, it pointed me in that direction. I surely wouldn't hang two in a row to the same guy.

Well, this one didn't hang, but it wasn't good, either, which annoyed me a lot and frightened me a little.

It broke to the inside corner. That was not the plan, and almost never was. My slider was supposed to look like a fastball, and the concept, when I threw it on the batter's side of the plate, was to start it in the vicinity of his body and make him bail out. If he were to bail and swing at the same time, which Stanley had been known to do and wasn't uncommon in the larger scheme of things—especially for power hitters always looking to yank a ball out of the park—the fat part of the bat would whistle through the inside corner of the plate. For my purposes, it was best if the ball were not right there when it did. So, as a rule, I wanted to miss inside, which would generally lead to a strike if the hitter swung and a ball—a *strategic* ball, one that set me up for the outside corner—if he didn't. If I screwed up and the pitch found the hitting zone and the batter swung, trouble had a way of ensuing.

I screwed up. Stanley didn't swing. Good man.

He did swing, however, at the fastball I subsequently brought on the outside corner. But as he made his bid, his bat head was not in total agreement with his back foot. This was working out.

At 0-and-2, the choice for the third pitch was pretty much guaranteed. I wouldn't waste it, but neither would I leave it in the zone. I'd make it look like a strike, which Stanley would probably swing at, and finish as a ball, which he probably wouldn't be able to hit. Having started him inside and successfully followed away, I'd now follow *farther* away. The slider, of course.

It ducked just off the corner, as it was supposed to, but Stanley held back, which he *wasn't* supposed to. And I'd thought I had a cooperative hitter on my hands. Swing at that! It looked good! What's wrong with you?

If Stanley wasn't willing to offer at a good slider, and I wasn't willing to offer him another bad one, that left the curve or the fastball. McCarver knew where I stood on that question: ties go to the fastball.

It was on the outside corner again—where else?—and a little higher than the previous one. Stanley reached, swung, and lifted the ball to Maris, who glided through the humidity to his left, well in front of the warning track, and gave the fourth inning a proper start.

TY COBB WAS the only Tiger—the only *man*—to win a batting title at a younger age than Al Kaline did. I would have liked to pitch to him. For one thing, I'd have been using a dead ball, and without the serious threat of a home run, pitching would induce less stress and enjoy more advantages. For another, Cobb was considered as mean and menacing a player as I was a pitcher—in fact, he might have me soundly beaten in that respect—and I'd be curious to find out if his reputation was more credible than mine. Either way, given our mutual enthusiasm for competition, it would have been an invigorating challenge. That said, I'd have enjoyed pitching to him even more if he'd been right-handed.

Thankfully, Kaline was. He was also, at thirty-three, thirteen years removed from his batting title. On the other hand, 1967 had been an All-Star year for him and one of his very best; and even in '68, when he'd broken his arm, he'd batted .309—a number that would have led the American League if it had covered the whole season—after returning to the lineup on the first of July.

Kaline was a studious hitter who made good use of the knowledge he gathered on the pitchers he faced. On me, obviously, he didn't have much to go on, just as I had little on him. There were a few right-handed hitters in the National League who approximated his ability to hit for both average and power, and a couple of those also played right field; but there wasn't a lot about Hank Aaron or Roberto Clemente that could be applied to anyone else. No other hitter was as quick as Aaron and there was none as creative as Clemente. I had so few answers for Aaron, who was the only right-handed batter that I typically pitched around, that I once broke out a knuckleball for him. He drilled it to Javier. Curt Simmons, a cagey left-hander whom I pitched alongside in the early sixties, drove Aaron crazy with change-ups; but mine didn't measure up to his—not even close—and I certainly didn't trust it against the likes of Henry. (When Aaron finally timed one of

Simmons's slowballs and clubbed it over the fence, he was called out for stepping on the plate.)

My best strategy for Clemente was to make him angry. He was well known for swinging at and often making good contact with anything thrown in the general neighborhood of home plate, but I was able to stretch his zone even farther by dusting him off early in the count. He'd pick himself up, squeeze finger grooves into his bat handle, and spin around flailing at fastballs and sliders beyond his reach. I should note that those pitches were not merely outside, but *low* and outside. If I got them *high* and outside, he'd make me wish he'd simply broken my leg again.

The outside-corner model was my bestseller overall, but there were a few great right-handed hitters that I pitched inside. I found it advisable, for instance, to make Willie Mays uncomfortable. Frank Robinson—I was a happy fellow when the Reds traded him to Baltimore—crowded the plate so fiercely that his elbow was a more compelling target than McCarver's mitt. And Joe Torre, who was later traded to the Cardinals and became one of my best friends—when he managed the New York Mets, he hired me as an "attitude coach"—handled the outside corner so well that I had no alternative but to work the other one.

Having no such history with Kaline, however, I stuck to the basics. His first time up, I'd started him with fastballs and struck him out on a slider away, so, keeping it simple, I came back to the slider away. He and Gorman agreed that it was too away, and probably low besides.

I tried it again, in the zone, and Kaline let it go for strike one.

I tried it *again*, in the zone—at least for a while—and this time he swung, to no avail.

It was the best stretch of the day for my slider. The break was late and sharp and double-sided, with plenty of depth and good destinations. And now, with two strikes by breaking balls, it didn't matter what I threw; the slider was working and the fastball was set up.

I stayed with the slider away but didn't get it close enough to make him swing. Two-and-two and time to move on.

The fastball that came next was a little too centered, but just high enough that Kaline fouled it back toward the NBC booth, where Harry Caray was caught without the net that he kept handy for our regular-season radio broadcasts. From what I'd seen, it was doubtful that he would've made the play anyway.

He might have had a better chance, though, at my second straight fastball. I lost my grip and it looped ridiculously high and off course, directly over Kaline's head. Al landed on his number 6—Musial's number, as well—and rolled right back up, then dusted his trousers and reassumed his position near the inside corner. He knew the pitch was unintentional.

And yet, it had happened, and the next pitch would play off it. That was the implied reality as McCarver rubbed the baseball, giving Kaline a moment to collect himself, and I walked to the grass to await his return throw.

This is where, as I reviewed the video almost half a century after the fact, I understood that on October 2, 1968, I was feeling and thinking and throwing just a little bit differently than I normally did. Because, as I watched myself regroup and listened to Harry and Curt Gowdy discuss my perspiration, I was *sure* another fastball was coming. I even said so. Guaranteed it. Kaline evidently thought the same thing, and McCarver must have called for one, because there I am in the faded footage, shaking him off with that little twitch of the head to the right. And then throwing a slider.

It didn't drop as much as the four sliders that preceded it, but it swerved abruptly to the outside corner, crossing just enough of it to send up Gorman's right hand. Kaline, the consummate pro, gave the ump the briefest of looks as he trudged back to the Tigers' dugout.

UMPIRES GIVE AND take. Gorman gave me a close call at the corner on the 3-2 pitch to Kaline, but he took a strike away on the first pitch to Norm Cash, a fastball on the outer half around the letters. Cash, standing deep in the batter's box, swiveled his hips and shoulders into it and checked his swing. Or didn't, in my view.

For the most part, though, I thought the umps did right by me in '68. And I think that's what happens when a pitcher is consistent with his location. Consistency on the corner was how my professional maturity presented itself. At thirty-two, I wasn't throwing quite as hard as I had at twenty-five or twenty-nine. And although my curveball had been effective against the Tigers, it hadn't been a big difference-maker during the season. Not in comparison to consistency on the corner.

I mentioned earlier that my control had been steadily improving throughout the decade, and if you look at my record, that improvement jumps off the page. Not just in the number of walks I allowed, although those figures certainly tracked my progress along those lines—1968 was the first and only season in which I permitted fewer than two bases on balls for every nine innings, down from more than five in 1961—but in the number of *wins*.

I'm well aware that this kind of thinking makes me hopelessly old-school, but I measured my personal progress with my win total. Winning is the point of pitching, after all, and while there certainly are elements of the outcome that you can't control—I've been moaning about my run support since statistics came out only in the *Sporting News* or the Sunday paper—the job is still about beating the guy in the other dugout. More than in my strikeouts or my ERAs, I took pride in the fact that, from '61 to '68, my victories increased every single year with the exception of 1967, when I missed eight starts with the gift from Clemente.

Ironically, though, 1967 became a turning-point season for me. When my broken leg had healed and I returned to the mound in September, I didn't push it too hard in my first game back, leaving with a lead after five innings. After that, I had four more starts in the regular season, followed by three in the World Series, and one by one they stamped out the frustrations of my downtime. I gave up more than one earned run only once during that stretch, and that was in our 7–2 victory in game seven of the Series.

Not long ago, over a nice bottle of wine, McCarver suggested to me that my '68 season had actually begun in those last seven games of '67. I hadn't thought of it that way, and I'd never admit it to his face, but I believe he's right. I don't know how to account for it, though, unless the late-season rest did me some good. Or maybe I was just pitching with a vengeance because sitting out a pennant race had me champing at the bit. Maybe it was because Johnny Keane had died that year and I wanted to do something special for him. Maybe, when I was on the shelf, I saw that the club could win without me and it took some of the burden off; made me less fearful of a costly mistake and in turn more aggressive. Or maybe it impelled me to validate my worth and reclaim my status. Most likely, my '67 surge had its roots in a few or all of those things. At any rate, my earned run average in that period was 0.76. If you start there and tack on

1968, it comes out to 1.06—an improvement over the 1.12 that I set the modern record with.

I pitched well out of the gate in '68, but not exceptionally so. The assassination of Dr. King was a blow. His funeral was held on April 9, the day most teams, including ours, were scheduled to start the season. The Pirates and a few others were actually due to open the day before, but Clemente took a public stand and persuaded his teammates not to play. At the same time, I made it clear that I wouldn't pitch until the service was over. Ultimately, all games were postponed until April 10, when I gave up one unearned run in seven innings against the Braves but didn't get a decision in a game we ultimately won 2–1.

In fact, I didn't earn a win until my last start of the month, which was my fourth, and didn't throw my first shutout until early June, on the day after Robert Kennedy was killed in a hotel kitchen after winning the California presidential primary. I won't say that the two events were unrelated. RFK's murder, coming two months after Dr. King's, hardened me. The slaying of Dr. King had touched me—and Flood and Brock and Clemente and millions of others across the country—on so many levels that anger competed against a squall of other emotions. This was different. Bobby Kennedy had become the front-runner to succeed Lyndon Johnson, who announced at the end of March that he wasn't seeking reelection, and when Kennedy met the same tragic fate that his brother had less than five years earlier, the anger rose to the top. At least for me. And I typically pitched my best when I was under its influence.

The June 6 shutout came on the road against the Astros, and it evened my record at 5–5. It also got me going on a two-month roll that came to resemble the historic one that Don Drysdale—a tall, side-wheeling, intimidating right-hander who'd been an

All-Star before Koufax overshadowed him in the Dodgers' rotation and was still one now, with Koufax retired—had just completed when he went a record 58 and two-thirds innings without giving up a run. After Houston, I put up zeros against the Braves, Reds (in an hour and 42 minutes), Cubs (1–0 over Ferguson Jenkins), and Pirates, and when I took the mound at Dodger Stadium on July 1, my streak of scoreless innings stood at 47. As it happened, my opponent was Drysdale. People were watching.

With two outs in the bottom of the first, I gave up a single to Len Gabrielson, then another to Tom Haller, which sent Gabrielson to third base and brought Ron Fairly to the plate. Fairly, a left-handed-batting first baseman, was a career .266 hitter, but you'd have never known it by the way he knocked me around. Year after year—until he came over to the Cardinals in my final season, when I learned that he purposely held his hands at the very top of the strike zone and wouldn't swing at a pitch above them—he might have been the toughest out on my dance card. And yet, he once had the gall to tell me that my stuff was so good he didn't know how anybody ever got a hit against me. This was while he was in the process of piling up more of them than any other player.

Naturally, Fairly concerned me as Gabrielson took his lead off third. I intended to keep the ball away from him, but overthrew a two-seamer that dipped inside. Johnny Edwards was catching that night, and the pitch caught him by surprise, glancing off the edge of his mitt. Gabrielson scooted home, the official scorer ruled it a wild pitch—which made the run earned and consequently ended my streak—and Drysdale's record had survived.

We won the game 5–1, and when we left Los Angeles we flew up the coast to San Francisco, where I squared off with Marichal—who, as if I weren't sufficiently motivated already, had 15 wins to my 10—and shut out the Giants. For two months, it seemed as though I was incapable of missing a corner, unless Ron Fairly was standing up there. Over that period, I shut out every team in the league except Fairly's damn Dodgers. For the 95 innings between the seventh of June 2 and the fourth of July 30, my earned run average worked out to 0.19.

I mention all this to make the point that the ball was coming out of my hand pretty well in 1968. The control of my backdoor slider, in particular, sort of completed me as a pitcher, if such a thing is possible. Rusty Staub, a polished left-handed hitter whom I respected and enjoyed competing with—a deluxe version of Fairly, he generally got the best of me until I figured out that he approached his at-bats backward, building toward a breaking ball that he could serve the other way—observed, correctly, that I no longer had to rely entirely on my fastball when I got behind in the count. I was also less prone *to get* behind in the count.

I wish I could offer a tidy explanation as to how I came by all that command. Koufax's control improved tremendously when he was convinced to ease up a bit, to not throw every pitch at maximum effort—to quit grunting, was how he looked at it. Nelson Briles started spotting the ball much better, and in my opinion became something of a trendsetter, when he switched to a no-windup delivery in 1967. I did neither of those things. As a rule, I tended to hold back just a little until I found myself in a tight spot against a dangerous hitter; but my basic motion was all-out all the time, which is why I flung myself toward the first-base line on every pitch. I had some spring in my legs—in high school, I set an Omaha record for the indoor high jump—and used that impetus as a source of power in throwing a baseball. I was never tempted to withhold that power. And I never refrained from grunting like a female tennis player when I pushed off the rubber. Many times, after a game, my throat would be sore from grunting so much and so hard.

So there was no obvious mechanical rationale for the increased frequency with which I was now able to dab the edges of the plate. I suppose it was simply maturation. Repetition. Muscle memory. Basically, time.

In August, I collected three more shutouts—the last of them coming on August 28, the worst day of rioting at the Democratic National Convention in Chicago—and extended my winning streak to 15 games. I started September with a 10-inning shutout of the Reds, we clinched the pennant in Houston on the 15th, with Steve Carlton doing the honors, and two days later, at Candlestick Park, I found myself on the wrong end of a no-hitter. It was perpetrated by Gaylord Perry, who got the game's only run when Ron Hunt, of all people, took me deep in the first inning, accounting for half his season's homers. Our revenge came the next night, when Ray Washburn no-hit the Giants right back (thanks in large part to a great catch by Flood on a shot hit into the gap by McCovey with two outs in the ninth). Vintage '68.

I lost again in my second-to-last game of the regular season, 3–2 to Don Sutton and the Dodgers, and it bumped my ERA from 1.13 to 1.16, two hundredths of a run behind the 1.14 that the great Walter Johnson rang up in 1913 to establish what was considered the modern record. While the shutout of the Astros on my final start pulled me past the Big Train, I was more pleased that it secured my 22nd victory, keeping alive the streak of increasing my win total every full season in which I didn't break a leg. Without that last win, I'm not sure I could have considered it a great season.

A great *regular* season, that is.

There was still the matter of the Tigers. And, more immediately, Norm Cash, with a count of 1-and-0, even though *he swung the damn bat!*

He swung more conspicuously at the next pitch, a fastball at the knees, and lifted it to Flood for the final out of the fourth.

IN HIS HOME state of North Dakota, Roger Maris remains the official record-holder for home runs in a season, in spite of Sammy Sosa, Mark McGwire, Barry Bonds, and the steroids era. The state senate saw to it by unanimously passing a resolution in 2005.

In both North Dakota and the world, Maris also holds the record for most kickoff returns for touchdown in one game, running back four of them on behalf of his Catholic high school in Fargo. He had a scholarship offer to play for Bud Wilkinson at Oklahoma, but the Cleveland Indians, whose policy it was to not allow a minor leaguer to play in his hometown, made an exception for Maris and kindly assigned him to Fargo-Moorhead (the two towns surround the border between North Dakota and Minnesota) to begin his professional baseball career. That kept him close to his high school sweetheart, who became his wife and mother of their six kids.

By way of both Cleveland and Kansas City, Roger landed with the Yankees in 1960, and played in his first World Series, in which he homered twice, later that year. The Series in '67, with us, was his sixth and best, with a .385 average and a team-record seven RBIs (although the World Series *play* he is best known for was the one against the Giants in 1962 when, with two outs in the bottom of the ninth inning of game seven, Matty Alou on first base, and the Yankees up 1–0, he cut off a shot by Mays down the right-field line, spun around, and delivered a strike to his relay man, Bobby Richardson, holding Alou at third; the next batter was McCovey, and the line drive he ripped, like Roger's throw, was a strike to Richardson).

Still sporting his familiar flattop, Maris came to us as the ultimate veteran, and played the role as well as he played right field. I know that McCarver, among others, benefited from Roger's practical wisdom. One night in Pittsburgh early in the '68 season, when Tim was still frustrated by his inability to demolish the new unbreakable helmets, he was jammed by Steve Blass, whom he knew he could hit, and grounded out weakly in a key situation. Furious but unable to satisfactorily punish his helmet, he carried it and our heavy lead bat into the raunchy bathroom in the old visitors' clubhouse at Forbes Field. Maris was already in there having a cigarette, and as Tim raised the bat to commence the final assault on his headgear, Roger said, "Do you know what would happen to this team if you hurt yourself?" That was all he had to say. Tim put the bat down and never endangered another batting helmet.

It's a fact of baseball that a player with Roger's credentials gets the attention of his teammates. Some of them fail to put that influence to good use, but Maris did, in his quiet way. His clout, I believe, had as much to do with his down-to-earth nature as with outslugging Mantle and beating Babe Ruth. It certainly wasn't a mere matter of mystique or awe, because most of us had been on the team that took care of his Yankees in '64. At the same time, though, we all recognized Roger as the quintessential been-there-done-that guy, whether it was setting records or being famous or playing in a lot of World Series. His humility only enhanced those accomplishments.

I suspect that the presence of Maris was enthusiastically welcomed even by Harry Caray. That's because, along with plenty of other reasons, Roger's famous 61st home run had come at the expense of a pitcher named Tracy Stallard, who was representing Boston at the time but came to the Cardinals in 1965 and ran afoul of our colorful play-by-play man. It started when Harry pointed out what a terrible fielder Stallard was and wondered on the air why teams didn't just bunt on him. When he'd had his fill of this, Stallard cut loose on Harry in an interview with the *St. Louis Globe-Democrat*. That was all pretty standard stuff, but then, one night in a lounge, Tracy's date spotted Harry across the room and asked Stallard to introduce them. So, affirming the stupidity of men in the presence of women, he went up to Harry and asked him to join them at their table. Harry told him to drop dead. After that, the two of them were content to steer clear of each other until, maybe a couple weeks later, Stallard pitched a three-hit shutout in Chicago. Naturally, Harry expected him afterward for the Star of the Game Show down on the field. When Tracy didn't show up, Harry fumed and fussed and bellowed, "Where the hell is Stallard?" As an ever-helpful teammate, I took it upon myself to dash into the clubhouse and inform Tracy that Harry needed him on the field. His response was, "Fuck Harry." So I hustled back to Harry with the important news: "Hey, Harry. Tracy says 'Fuck you.'" I truly believe that, if he hadn't had a show to do, Harry would have stormed the clubhouse and tried to fight Stallard, who stood six-foot-five and weighed more than two hundred pounds. Stallard wasn't quite as incapacitated, though, and in spite of his message he did indeed come out to see Harry. They screamed at each other for a while, and I left Wrigley Field with a smile on my face.

At any rate, Maris was roundly appreciated in St. Louis. And yet, as highly as I thought of him, and as extraordinary as he'd been in the early sixties, I can understand that his great years weren't quite numerous enough to get him into the Hall of Fame. I was pleased, however, that he made it onto a postage stamp in 1999.

And I was pleased, on this Indian summer afternoon of 1968, when he started the bottom of the fourth with a walk.

On four pitches. All fastballs. All high.

CEPEDA NOW. BALL one, high.

Ball two, inside.

And out came Mayo Smith to talk with McLain, to get him to stop overthrowing, to assure him, maybe, that Cepeda wasn't the hitter he'd been the year before as the MVP. He certainly wasn't the hitter he'd been in 1961, the year the guy who'd be leading off first base when the meeting was over and the guy who'd be holding him on had led the American League in home runs, of course, and average, respectively, while Cha Cha led the National with 46 homers and 142 RBIs.

They were all connected, like so many ballplayers are. In less than four years, McLain and Cepeda would be traded for each other. When Maris made the great play that saved the Yankees in 1962, it was Cepeda, following McCovey in the Giants' lineup, who would otherwise have led off the tenth inning of a tie game. Maris and Cepeda, the meat of our batting order—two guys who blended beautifully into the ball club even though their personalities couldn't have been more different—were both playing their last series for the Cardinals, and while we all knew Roger was retiring, who would have guessed that, less than a week before the next Opening Day, Orlando would be traded to the Braves for Joe Torre?

Now, as Smith returned to the dugout and Maris took his sidesteps off the base and McLain barely peeked at him under the pulled-down brim of his cap and Cash didn't bother to offer his pitcher an obligatory target and a kid sitting near the NBC booth hollered, "Come on, Cha Cha, hit it out of here," Cepeda, in his customary closed stance, bounced musically on his aching knees. And swung at what might have been ball three, high again, fouling it back.

Those were magnificent lineups he'd been such a big part of in San Francisco, and after pitching against the Giants, year after year—not to mention the Braves (Aaron, Torre, Eddie Mathews, Joe Adcock, Rico Carty, Felipe Alou), the Reds (Frank Robinson, Vada Pinson, Lee May, Rose, Perez), and even the Cubs (Billy Williams, Ernie Banks, Ron Santo)—I wasn't about to shrink at the sight of the Tigers, as deep and formidable as they were; just as, for the same reason, I hadn't been intimidated by the Yankees in '64 or the Red Sox in '67. Cepeda had something to do with that.

He took another high fastball; 3-and-1. McLain stood frozen for a moment, disgusted with himself and in danger of walking a second straight batter to open the inning. After wandering about for a few beats, he then served up a high, fat fastball that might well have put us ahead if Orlando had been fresh and fully healthy. He fouled it back.

McLain had thrown Cepeda five sidearm pitches the first time around, and now came another one. It was at the upper, outer reaches of the strike zone and Cha Cha, too slow, popped it up just foul of first base, where, as the 1961 home run champion returned to the bag, the 1961 batting average champion retired the 1961 RBI champion.

IN THE SECOND inning, before wriggling out of trouble, McLain had learned that McCarver was a very good breaking-ball hitter. So he now brought the fastball and did with it what he'd been repeatedly doing: threw it high. Ball one.

We were probably seeing the effect of those 336 innings Denny had pitched during the regular season. Fatigue messes with control and encourages overthrowing, no matter how many Pepsi-Colas go down the hatch to fight it off. When you mix in the effort McLain had expended to survive the second and third, and the frequent battles from behind in the count—on top of a sore shoulder, the stuffy air, and the extra strain of the stakes involved—we were facing a pitcher who was primed for roughing up. On the other hand, our distinguished opponent was also possessed of a highly developed talent for mastering situations, as attested by 31 victories and the first three innings.

Another high fastball and another 2-0 count, the third in a row. McLain dropped a hand to one hip and his glove on the other. Maybe Tim wouldn't even have to swing that baby bat of his, and Shannon would get another crack at an RBI.

Ball three was well outside. McLain turned around and shook his head. For the season, he had averaged fewer than two walks for every nine innings. Now he was a pitch away from the second one in *this* inning.

Ball four, high.

And here we go again.

WHEN HE WAS a twenty-four-year-old rookie outfielder, Mike Shannon had tied game one of the 1964 World Series—a game and a Series we would go on to win—with a two-run homer off Whitey Ford, the winningest pitcher in World Series history. From then on, we knew he'd be up to the task in times like these.

Four years later, Shannon was counting on a big postseason in one way or another. For weeks, he'd been jabbering about our trip to Japan after the Series and going on about how he was going to hunt down a black bear with a crossbow. None of the rest of us knew there were black bears in Japan; but then, there wasn't much overlap between Moon Man's sphere of knowledge and everybody else's. As it turned out, his crossbow was confiscated at the Japanese airport. We were stuck at security for hours while they tried to figure out what the hell he had there.

But you couldn't stay mad at Shannon. He'd do anything for the ball club, and to get in the lineup. Third base wasn't the first new position he'd agreed to try. In 1965, when both McCarver and Bob Uecker were hurt, he even put on the catcher's gear, with a little assistance. To Shannon, anything was better than sitting on the bench. In 1966, when he was sharing time in the outfield with Bobby Tolan and Alex Johnson—don't get me started on *him*—Mike was so disappointed that he seriously thought about going back to football. The Atlanta Falcons were actually interested in him.

The move to third was good for both Shannon and the Cardinals. Stan Musial was our general manager in '67, and I'm sure it meant a lot to Mike—growing up in St. Louis as he did, he revered Musial—when Stan said that Shannon's embrace of his new role set up the whole championship season. In '68, he came up even bigger.

That was why I'd expected Moon Man to put us ahead in the second inning, when he had the chance, and his failure to do so didn't prevent me from expecting it again, with two on and one out.

He looked as though *he* expected it, too, standing close to the plate, loose and calm, choked up an inch or so on the bat. Not many players Shannon's size choke up anymore; not many players of any size do, with the ballparks smaller and the salaries bigger and home runs being the most cashable of base hits. I suspect that the onslaught of stand-alone statistics might have something to do with it, as well. And the advice of agents. A lot of players don't even choke up or somehow modify their approaches to protect the plate with two strikes, which I don't understand. They're up there taking the same big swings at pitches less likely to be where they're swinging, making themselves easier outs. In 1968, major-league batters struck out 5.9 times every nine innings. In 2014, they struck out 7.7 times, an increase of nearly 33 percent. I think I could make a living wage in that environment.

Shannon took strike one on the outside corner, the best pitch McLain had thrown in the inning.

The next one, delivered sidearm, might have been even better. It arrived in the vicinity of Shannon's collarbone and sent him sprawling.

McLain may or may not have intended to knock him down—I'd go with not, since it would have loaded the bases if Mike had sprawled less effectively and gotten himself hit—but the level of intent was immaterial. What was relevant was the *next* pitch, which, in light of the previous one, stood an excellent chance of coming sidearm and angling for the outer half. Freehan evidently wasn't thinking along those lines, but McLain was, shaking off two signs before spotting a sidearm fastball on the outer half. Shannon reached and fouled it harmlessly.

At 1-2 now, needing contact to advance Maris or bring him home, Shannon added another inch or so to his choke-up. That subtle adjustment might have made a critical difference when he checked his swing on the next high fastball.

By extending the confrontation, the checked swing itself most definitely made a critical difference when, on 2-2, McLain dropped down sidearm once more and our intrepid bear hunter shot a single through the hole to Stanley's right.

Maris cut the corner at third base, and Willie Horton, in left field, must have thought he had a chance to throw Roger out at the plate. He charged hard, reached down, and came up empty. The ball rolled behind him ten feet or so, enough to allow Mc-Carver to steam into third and Shannon into second as Maris scored easily.

I honestly don't recall whether Flood looked at me and said, "There's your run, big guy." But the odds are good that he did.

WITH RUNNERS ON second and third, the Tigers brought their infielders a couple steps closer to the plate. That was expected. So was a breaking ball or something sidearm to Javier. McLain had put those two things together to strike him out, looking, in a similar spot in the second inning.

The sidearm twist must have really thrown Hoolie off, because he normally hacked in futility at bending, right-handed pitches like that. Our bullpen coach, Bob Milliken, had worn himself out throwing curveballs to Javier in the hope that he'd stop bailing and flailing at the sight of them. It was a perpetual cause on our club. At one point, the Cardinals actually believed that

Javier's new wraparound glasses might give him a better look at the slow, swooping stuff that seemed to discombobulate him every time. Nothing helped much.

If McLain were to walk Javier, it would load the bases with one out but bring the batting order to Maxvill and me, which wasn't a bad option for him. A bad option—almost an inconceivable option to those of us who over the years had observed the good Hoolie and the bad Hoolie taking turns in the batter's box, swapping in and out according to the degree of wrinkle in the pitch—was an overhand fastball over the heart of the plate. When that very thing came his way, before anything else, Javier was able to contain his excitement, control his swing, and skip it a few inches to the right of Cash, who likely would have made a play if he'd been stationed at his normal depth. The ball was hit hard enough that, if Cash had snared it between skips, McCarver might have held at third, which of course would have kept Shannon at second. As it was, even though Mike's leadoff was limited because McLain had pitched from the stretch, he also scored, sliding in ahead of a strong throw from Kaline.

It was quite a moment, and if it seems as though I'm going out of my way to portray it as lucky for us, it's because lucky—like I'd won the lottery—is how three runs made me feel in 1968. *Three runs!*

Hooray for Hoolie!

JAVIER MASSAGED HIS right knee as he stood on first base, but on ball two to Maxvill—the sixth straight ball McLain had thrown Maxie over two plate appearances—he broke for second and stole it easily when Freehan's throw, which was late anyway, drifted to the right. Then he called time and walked off toward center field, lifting, bending, and grabbing his knee along the way. No coach. No trainer. No problem, apparently. Back to the bag.

Between the two of them, Javier and Maxvill would play twenty-three seasons as defensive aces in the middle of the Cardinals' infield. They would then serve as pillars of baseball in their home communities. For Javier, that involved nurturing the game back in the Dominican Republic; for Maxvill, it meant staying home to coach the Cardinals—alongside Red Schoendienst, when Ken Boyer was the manager—and ultimately run the club for ten years as general manager, starting with the World Series season of 1985.

As little as those guys—especially Maxvill—hit, they represented at least three of the underlying basics that characterized the Cardinals in those days. We caught the ball. We ran the bases. And, to an uncommon degree, we were made up of quality people who not only created a constructive atmosphere— among other things, our racial camaraderie was way ahead of the curve—but left their marks on the game. McCarver, of course, would attain fame as one of its more renowned television analysts. Shannon, in his folksy style that only a hometown could love, has been a St. Louis broadcasting icon for more than forty years, since health problems forced him to retire prematurely as a player at the age of thirty-one. Nelson Briles, a well-balanced, interesting guy, was also a popular announcer. Cepeda, Brock, and Carlton are all in the Hall of Fame. Maris has been immortalized in legend, books, and films. And Flood, of course, became the martyr of player rights when he sacrificed his career by refusing a trade and challenging the reserve clause.

It was that way, in fact, through most of my seventeen years with the ball club. My earlier teammates included Musial, the ultimate Cardinal and one of the sport's most beloved figures for the half century between his retirement and death; Boyer, who managed the Cardinals for parts of three years; Bill White, who advanced to the presidency of the National League; and Bob Uecker, the game's leading comedian. Among the later ones were Torre, who holds an influential position in the commissioner's office in the wake of a celebrated managing career that included four World Series titles with the Yankees; Ted Simmons, a former GM of the Pirates and executive for several teams; and the Mad Hungarian, Al Hrabosky, who, after carving out his niche as a relief pitcher who talked to the baseball, has been talking into a microphone for more than thirty years as the color commentator on the Cardinals' television broadcasts.

Almost to a man, the game was important to us, on both the macro and micro levels. Our heads were in it.

That being the case, I expected Maxvill to take a pitch on 2-and-0, considering that he hadn't seen a strike from McLain all day. It might also have been a good idea to extend the at-bat a while longer and afford Javier some extra time to work out the kinks in his knee. But when the ball arrived on the inside corner from the sidearm slot, Maxie lifted it to Horton in left for the second out.

THE YEAR BEFORE, when we'd opened the Series in Boston, Schoendienst had sent out the very same lineup that McLain was facing. Jose Santiago had been the pitcher for the Red Sox, and I'd had a chance to put us in front in the second inning, with one out and the bases loaded. I grounded into a double play. My next time up—after Santiago had dinged me for a home run to tie the game at one apiece—I had *another* chance to put us ahead, with two outs in the fourth inning and Javier on second, just like now. I struck out.

I did homer off Jim Lonborg in game seven, and I could tell myself that McLain was more like Lonborg than Santiago. I could also flatter myself with the notion that he was showing me respect—*fear,* baby!—with a first-pitch slider that slid outside for ball one. Or maybe it was a cut fastball, because the second pitch was definitely a slider and, unlike the first one, it broke sharply downward. I swung over it.

He was unloading his arsenal on me. At 1-and-1, he dropped down sidearm for a fastball that stayed high. Then another sidearm fastball that bored inside. I bounced it foul, wide of third base.

Now it was all about making contact. Funky knee or not, Javier would score if I could just dump a ball behind an infielder. McLain wouldn't want the count to reach 3-and-2, a ball away from Brock coming to the plate, so I'd almost certainly get a pitch I could put the bat on. I was thinking something from over the top. Something hard and straight.

Sidearm. Slider.

Swing and miss.

Not such a terrible thing, actually. It enabled me to head back to the mound angry, in spite of three runs.

	1	2	3	4	5	6	7	8	9	R	H	E
Tigers	0	0	0	0						0	2	2
Cardinals	0	0	0	3						3	3	0

(AP Photo)

When he wasn't discombobulated by a slider, as he was here, Willie Horton could clobber a ball as hard and far as any batter in the game. In 1968, he put that power on display with 36 home runs, tied for second in all of baseball. Willie was both a native and a favorite of Detroit.

Fifth Inning

I HAD WILLIE Horton just where I wanted him: leading off. That meant, of course, that he'd bat with nobody on base. And with a fresh three-run lead, I could pitch more aggressively and challenge him in the strike zone, knowing that the worst-case result would be a *two*-run lead.

A pitcher with good stuff, having the advantage of being able to succeed over a wider portion of home plate—here ya go, pal!—should benefit more from a decent lead than one who has to nibble and deceive; and I'd like to say that any three-run cushion was safe in my custody. Unfortunately, that wasn't the case. In a late August game against the Pirates, we'd gone ahead 3–0 by scoring three times in the bottom of the fourth—sound familiar?—and I'd responded by giving up *six* from the seventh inning on.

The Tigers, furthermore, had bludgeoned the American League with late-inning comebacks, and the power pack in front of me, with his cartoon forearms, was their leading bludgeoner. So, overconfidence was out of the equation. Good judgment was in, if I could stumble upon some.

But good judgment, to me, in this scenario, involved resisting the temptation to be passive or the slightest bit content with a three-run lead. There would be no letting up, no backing off, no slowing down. When you're out in front, with runs to work with, you keep it coming. You finish the job. You put the pedal to the metal.

Concerning Horton, meanwhile, I reasoned that I'd gained a quick upper hand the first time around—he was late on the fastball and unprepared for the breaking pitch—and the exercise now was to keep him uncomfortable as long as possible. To that end, I started him with a slider on the outer half. He went for it, and popped it to Javier on the edge of the grass. I was on pace to tie a major-league record with a three-pitch inning.

First-pitch swinging has lost favor with conventional wisdom, and I was certainly delighted to chalk up an out with so little wear and tear; but Horton had his reasons, evidently, and I can appreciate them. He figured correctly that, flushed with a sudden lead, I'd come out throwing strikes. And even though his aggressiveness hadn't been immediately rewarded, I'd have to be wary of it the next time he stepped to the plate. I'd have to think twice about expanding my workspace to include more of the zone.

Conversely, if I could be reasonably sure that a batter would take the first pitch, I was more than happy to accept his generosity and get ahead in the count. He was, in effect, putting me in charge of the round—dropping his gloves and sticking his chin out. When that happened, *I* was the one who came out swinging. First-pitch hitting, I believe, would make a rapid comeback if modern pitchers were more devoted to first-strike pitching. In the Dark Ages, we were taught to go after the batter and put a strike on the board in advance of ball one. I later coached that philosophy, and nothing has persuaded me to back away from it. There were certain batters whom I pitched around in certain situations, but, for me and most old-school pitchers, avoiding the plate was not a general practice early in the count. I was in hot pursuit of strike one, and I found that if I happened, accidentally, to make a first-pitch fastball a little friendlier than I'd meant to, most of the time the batter fouled it back. Nowadays that pitch would frequently be taken. The result is technically the same, but *effectively* it's not, because it eases the pitcher's fear of throwing strikes out of the gate. For the hitter, the emphasis has turned to working the pitcher and getting deep in the count, and while that makes good sense in theory, and is a great idea if the pitcher is reluctant to attack the strike zone, I see it as an invitation to put the first pitch over the plate. And I thank you.

Not too long ago, after years of watching Derek Jeter come up big in the playoffs and World Series, I mentioned to him one day that I'd noticed something: while he almost always let the first pitch go by during the regular season, he often didn't do that in the postseason. And he hit some home runs that way.

He just looked at me and smiled. Didn't say a word.

I SUPPOSE THAT Jim Northrup, as much as anyone, was typical of the guys on the other side.

He grew up following the Tigers (in Breckenridge, Michigan, near the center of the state).

He came from a multisport background (and starred in *five* of them at Alma College).

He didn't mind fighting. (There was the McLain squabble over cards, and the charge of the mound in Oakland.)

He appreciated McLain as a pitcher and musician (and pretty much left it at that).

And he was diligent about his craft. (Once, after a disappointing game, he called the general manager at one o'clock in the morning to ask if he could get the stadium lights turned on for extra batting practice.)

Being a left-handed batter with a pretty good idea of what he was up to, Northrup was probably the closest thing the Tigers had to Ron Fairly. His hero and hitting model was Ted Williams; but Fairly, in average, power, and style, was a more realistic comparison. Northrup, however, exceeded Williams at one aspect of hitting: stroking the ball to the opposite field. For that, he used the inside-out method that I'd seen Curt Flood prosper with. Williams, by contrast, was so uninterested in going the other way that he ignored Ty Cobb's written advice encouraging it and inspired early editions of the pull-side defensive shifts that, generations later, have made such an impact on the game. The tendency to hit the ball where it was pitched indicated that Northrup didn't ordinarily swing for the fences, which made his grand-slam outburst in 1968 all the more impressive. His power was genuine, and complemented a solid all-around approach. The package, as a whole, added up to a hitter with potential to give me some trouble.

Having struck out Northrup with a backdoor slider in the second inning, I figured he'd be looking for another—if not now, at some point. I decided to stick with the location but change the pitch, bringing a fastball that was too wide for McCarver to flag down.

Northrup's stance was slightly open—not nearly as extreme as McAuliffe's—and although he stood near the plate I expected him to be stepping toward it to cover the outside corner. I wanted to temper his aggressiveness by switching between inside and outside; but the next two-seamer split the difference. It dipped low enough, though, that Northrup fouled it between McCarver's knees and against Gorman's foot. Gorman hopped around for a few moments, then reset himself over Tim's right shoulder and called ball two on a fastball that sailed inside.

Northrup was now ahead, 2-and-1, and could afford to commit himself and take a rip. He'd most likely be counting on another fastball, and one that he could pull with power. Forget that. He got the fastball, and snapped his hips to yank it, but it was a pretty good one that stayed down and just out of his sweet spot. He fouled it straight back. That was *still* happening a lot. It tends to when the fastball has movement on it.

Since the slider on the outside corner that he'd swung and missed for strike three the last time up, Northrup hadn't seen a breaking pitch. He had to be thinking about that. But I wanted to move off the fastball at least once; so, while I was generally reluctant to throw the slider *inside* to a left-hander, I made an exception. I actually made two exceptions because, when I did throw the slider inside, I usually kept it on the hitter's hands, where it was harder to reach with the bat head. This one, however, bent low, off the plate. Full count; my fourth of the game.

But I liked the look of that pitch—Northrup appeared uncertain as it tumbled toward his feet—and doubled down. Northrup, with his sight lines adjusted, liked the look of *this* one, and as it carried to his knees he waited patiently, countering with his nifty inside-out, opposite-field swing.

The ball was well hit, but not beyond the reach of Maxvill, who rose in the air and caught it with two hands. A sign of the times.

———

IN 1967 AND again in 1968, both of them seasons in which he'd finished in the top three of his league's MVP voting, Bill Freehan had played in 155 ball games, an impressive number for a catcher. He didn't actually *catch* all of those, but he led his team in appearances and caught the great majority, the whole time battling through a nagging back injury, sustained in 1965, that eventually led to surgery on his spine in 1970. Freehan had been described as "a thinking man's catcher," but he was a working man's catcher, as well. And a tough cookie.

He was also a tough out, as I'd learned back in the second inning, when he cost me ten pitches. When he came to the plate with two outs in the fifth, I was glad to see his shirt drenched in sweat; glad, that is, to see that it worked both ways. Welcome to St. Louis, incidentally.

Although the long previous at-bat had not ended well for Freehan, it hadn't weakened his patience. He took a fastball a smidgen high or inside, and then a slider just a little bit low, to get ahead of me 2-and-0.

I wasn't eager to walk him—there was no call for extreme caution—but was less enthusiastic about pitching to his power when I didn't have to. A walk would leave him still a long way from scoring, with the bottom of the order to follow and only one out to get.

And yet, neither of us was willing to give in. When the third pitch arrived a tad high or tight, I wasn't sure which, Freehan checked his swing.

He was proving once again that he was admirably stubborn, and a guy I could relate to, even though he'd played in the Big Ten. (I'd wanted very much to do the same with a basketball scholarship to Indiana, which, under Branch McCracken, won the NCAA championship in my senior year of high school. Our coach wrote McCracken a letter on my behalf, but when the reply finally came it said that the Hoosiers had already filled their quota for Negroes.) At any rate, I'd go so far as to say that, with his strength of mind, character, and body—and I don't mean to imply that I wished for anyone other than McCarver to catch me, because I didn't—Freehan would have made an excellent Cardinal if he weren't such a Detroit Tiger through and through.

He would end up playing all fifteen of his big-league seasons in his hometown, to which he was clearly partial. After growing up in the Detroit suburbs and moving at age fifteen to St. Petersburg, Florida, when his father bought a business there, he would come back in the summers to stay with his grandparents and play ball for his Michigan teams. One of them won a national tournament when he was eighteen, and Freehan was named its MVP, although when he accepted the award he said his teammate, Willie Horton, was more deserving. He was an all-state quarterback in Florida, but came back again to play football and baseball at Michigan, where he later coached the baseball team. He finished college after he was drafted because his father said he couldn't touch his bonus money until he did.

Freehan and Horton would eventually team up not only on the Tigers for fourteen years but on four American League All-Star squads, the last of which, in 1973, represented Freehan's tenth straight selection out of the eleven he'd be recognized with. The man was a player.

But that's not why I walked him with my fourth pitch, a fastball down and away. I just did.

———

I WOULD NOT, however, walk Don Wert. I just wouldn't.

The only All-Star Game he would make was not on account of his hitting. And I felt pretty strongly that the only hitting he would do against me would come on lame sliders like the one he'd smacked for a single in the third inning. He wasn't getting another one of *those*.

He was getting a fastball on the outer half.

A swing, and strike one.

When Mayo Smith was studying ways to get Kaline into the Tigers' lineup for the World Series without removing Northrup or Stanley, he'd seriously considered switching his certain Hall of Famer to third base in place of Wert, who had batted under .200 in the months after being hit in the head. An obvious drawback to that plan was the possibility that Brock, in spite of his reluctance to bunt, might see fit to do so with a thirty-three-year-old outfielder playing third base, and Flood most certainly would. It might even give Javier a solid option against a right-hander. Furthermore, Wert had built up more equity than Ray Oyler, the guy next to him on the left side of Detroit's infield, and was still a more legitimate threat with the bat. The case for keeping Oyler in place, meanwhile, was based on the viable argument that a serviceable shortstop is much harder to approximate than any other infielder. But Smith believed he had something special in Stanley, whose athletic ability and general baseball proficiency emboldened his manager to hazard the experiment. So Oyler sat down, Stanley stepped in, and Wert retained his position.

And swung and missed another fastball on the outside corner.

At that point, Eddie Mathews emerged from the Tigers' dugout with a bat in his hands. If Wert happened to reach base, as he had before with two strikes on him, would they really pinch-hit for McLain this early in the game? It was a loaded scenario, and not just because McLain was the ace of the American League. Mathews, who had just completed his seventeenth and final regular season with 512 career homers—sixth on the all-time list, one more than Mel Ott and two ahead of his longtime teammate, Hank Aaron—would represent the tying run if he came to the plate in this inning. I advised myself not to go there.

Normally, this would have been the spot for a slider breaking just out of the zone, in the interest of a swinging strike three. Wert, instead, got another fastball on the outside corner for a looking strike three.

Although I wasn't counting or aware of it, the strikeout happened to be my ninth, the same number I had after five innings of the first Series game in Boston the year before. I finished that day with 10.

I HATE TO think what kind of trouble Brock would have caused me over the years if he'd remained with the Cubs, batting ahead of Billy Williams, Ernie Banks, and Ron Santo. It would have put four Hall of Famers within five slots of the batting order.

He wasn't giving McLain much difficulty, however, mostly because McLain, reprieved, was showing him pitches like the first one in the bottom of the fifth, a looping curveball that Lou, waiting, waiting, out of rhythm, fouled off to the left.

And the second one, a moving fastball away that Brock—keep your head in there, Lou!—pulled off just a bit as he swung hard and missed.

And the third one, a slider on the hands that Lou hit off the handle and bounced easily to Wert for the first out.

McLain was having similar success with Flood, which was generally a good way to beat us. The best Cardinal teams always seemed to thrive on small ball and scrappiness, which we got plenty of from Brock and Flood.

We weren't the second coming of the Gas House Gang, by any means, but that club, featuring Pepper Martin, Frankie Frisch, Joe Medwick, Rip Collins, Leo Durocher, and Paul and Dizzy Dean, had carved out the brand that we still represented thirty-four years later. Its legacy was made in 1934, when the Cardinals rallied from seven games back in early September and passed the New York Giants on the final two days of the season to earn a spot in the World Series, where, in seven games, they knocked off Detroit, which starred Mickey Cochrane, Hank Greenberg, Charlie Gehringer, Goose Goslin, and Schoolboy Rowe.

The Gas House connection and the Tigers-Cardinals thing were natural themes for the '68 Series; but the most conspicuous link was Dizzy Dean himself. At the time, Dean was closing out his long broadcasting career, which was highlighted by his extra-colorful commentating—singing "Wabash Cannonball" and popularizing such folksy phrases as "slud into third"—on the *Game of the Week* telecasts for CBS. He made the rounds in that job, and I'd met him a time or two, but I can't say that we had much in common, other than wearing the bat and birds on our chests, winning the MVP award in a pennant year divisible by 34, and throwing hard with the right hand.

Ironically, the more relevant comparisons were between Dizzy and McLain. The obvious correlation was winning 30 games, which I never did—which nobody but Dean and McLain has done since 1931—but the similarities carried far beyond that. To start with, both of them were twenty-four years old when they won 30 and pitched their teams to the World Series. (After the debilitating toe injury Dean suffered in the 1937 All-Star Game—"Fractured, hell; the damn thing's broken!"—he appeared in a second Series with the Cubs in 1938.)

Both of them transcended baseball; or at least made every effort to. While McLain played the lounges and cavorted with TV stars, Dean and brother Paul had breakfast with Will Rogers and Damon Runyon the moment they arrived in Detroit for the Series. On the morning of game one, Henry Ford sent a limo to pick up the Deans and bring them out to his museum and historic village in Dearborn. Dizzy idolized Ford, and Ford, in turn, told Dizzy that he'd done more to bring the world out of the dumps—this was during the Depression—than anyone else in any walk of life.

Both McLain and Dean appeared on the cover of *Time* magazine. And although McLain, a consummate sharpie, was certainly not the country bumpkin that Dean, raised in northeast Arkansas, portrayed himself to be—McLain's roommate would answer the hotel phone with "Denny McLain Enterprises, Ray Oyler speaking"—they shared a stage presence and force of personality. McLain was not a "Wabash Cannonball" kind of guy, but once, after pitching the first game of a doubleheader, he headed upstairs during the second, asked the organist to move aside, and serenaded the crowd with "Satin Doll."

In spite of his infamous favor to Mantle, McLain was less deferential to the other batters he addressed. "Okay, you big shithead," he told Frank Howard, "I'm gonna pitch you inside, right to your strength." Dean was like that, too, only funnier. During workouts on the day before the '34 Series opened, he walked up to home plate as Greenberg took batting practice, playfully shoved him aside, stepped into the box with a fungo bat, in his street clothes, with the cameras blazing, and instructed the pitcher to toss him a few, which he hammered into the outfield. Then he, Paul, and Pepper Martin broke into a war dance. At one point, Diz asked Greenberg if he'd like to touch the arm of a 30-game winner. For free.

Like Denny and me, Dean had a World Series counterpart. The Tigers' ace, Schoolboy Rowe, was also twenty-four and also from Arkansas—in fact, he was born in El Dorado, the same small town that produced Lou Brock. Rowe stood six-foot-four and pitched with good-luck charms in his pocket. One game, he stuffed his trousers with trinkets from several countries and at least a couple critters. After losing, he tossed them all out the window of his hotel room.

Dean won the first game of the Series, and as Rowe warmed up before the second, Dizzy sauntered up beside him and offered advice on which pitches would or wouldn't succeed against the Cardinals. He also bestowed a facetious compliment on Detroit's 24-game winner, marveling that Schoolboy could throw as hard with the wind as brother Paul—a twenty-one-year-old rookie who had won 19 games—could throw against it. Finally, Mickey Cochrane, the Tigers' catcher and manager, told him to scram. Cochrane could not be counted among Dizzy's admirers; or Paul's, either. He'd been playing the saxophone one night at the Detroit Athletic Club when he was asked for remarks on the upcoming Series and replied, "Bring on the Deans. I say to hell with them."

Dizzy was nearly as proud of his brother as he was of himself. The two—"me an' Paul"—were inseparable, and had been since they were young boys. They claimed that their pitching talents became evident when they killed squirrels with rocks; Paul would knock them out of the trees and Dizzy would do the deed. "God gave us perfect pitchin' builds," Paul said, "long and loose like hound dogs. We never ate no special victuals or nothin' like that to put speed in our soupbones—just lucky fellas to be born great pitchers."

In September of '34, Dizzy posted a shutout in the first game of a doubleheader and Paul followed with a no-hitter in the second, which prompted Dizzy to say that, hell, he'd have thrown a no-hitter, too, if he'd known what Paul had in store. Between them, the Deans pitched five of the Cardinals' final six games of the regular season, including the last three, which were all victories, two of them shutouts by Dizzy. When Paul carried the club past the Giants, into first place by themselves, on the second-to-last day, Dizzy led his teammates in a snake dance by the dugout. (McLain was not quite as public a celebrator, but after winning his 30th game, he did go out the next day and buy a Ford, a Chevy, and a Chrysler.)

Dizzy won the season finale on one day of rest, and as five policemen escorted him off the field, a young boy placed a cake of ice on the pitching rubber. The kid explained that, before the game, Dizzy had told him to do so, because the "this slab would be burnin' up, and he wasn't foolin'."

THE 1934 WORLD Series was the first covered by commercial radio. The sponsor happened to be Henry Ford's motor company.

Schoolboy Rowe, like Dizzy Dean, had started the last game of the regular season. Dizzy went the distance that day—the Sunday before the Series opened on Wednesday—but since the Tigers had already clinched the American League pennant, Rowe was excused after three innings. Nevertheless, he was held back until game two of the World Series. Dizzy's opponent in game one was thirty-five-year-old Alvin "General" Crowder, who wasn't really a general but *was* a World War I veteran who had served in the Philippines and Siberia. Crowder's service time was marked by two things that would distinguish his future: he learned to play baseball and had his right (pitching) arm adorned, elbow to shoulder, with a tattoo of a naked lady. He was, of course, no match for Diz.

Rowe took advantage of his extra day off, working all 12 innings of the Tigers' 3–2 victory in the second game. Paul Dean—sometimes known as Daffy, though he didn't care for it—put the Cardinals back ahead in game three 4–1, but, after winning game four, Detroit grabbed the advantage when Dizzy was beaten 3–1 in game five. Brother Paul, however, bested Rowe 4–3 in game six, and the Series came down to Dizzy and a young submarining Kansan named Elden Auker, known by his manager as Mule Ears.

Auker had won game four, but in game seven he was gone before the third inning was completed. In the sixth, with a lopsided score, Joe Medwick tripled and engaged in a little rumpus with the Tigers' third baseman, Marvin Owen. After the half inning had ended, the Detroit fans, seizing the opportunity to strike back at a team of bullies and blowhards (as they perceived the Cardinals, taking their cue from the baseball writers), pelted Medwick with produce, bottles, and other disposable items as he tried to take his position in left field. The game was delayed while a stadium crew picked up the debris and Medwick, steering clear of the fusillade, tossed the ball behind his back to Pepper Martin, who returned it by popping it off his upper arm. Finally the commissioner, Kenesaw Mountain Landis, called over Medwick, Owen, the managers, and umpire Bill Klem, and concluded his hearing by ordering Medwick off the field for his own protection.

The final was 11–0, with Dean throwing in a single and double and needing only 99 pitches, 76 of which were strikes, to finish his shutout. He struck out only five batters, but three of them were Greenberg. The last of those came in the ninth inning, on a fruitless swing at a pitch considerably outside, and it caused Dizzy to double over, hands on knees, laughing heartily.

"He'd cut the inside corner," said Goose Goslin, "then throw one at your knees and then brush off your shirt. He was the greatest that day I ever faced."

In the Series aftermath, a New York writer named Dan Daniel referred to the Cardinals, for the first time, as the gas house gang. The capital letters came later.

FROM MY PERSPECTIVE, any resemblance we bore to the Gas House Gang was based on a quieter, more refined model of its backbone and savvy. We didn't self-promote or mock the other team. Other than Cepeda—well, maybe Shannon—our nicknames were nothing like Dizzy, Daffy, Ducky, Dazzy, Ripper, the Lip, the Fordham Flash, Wild Bill, or the Wild Horse of the Osage. My similarities to Dizzy Dean were confined to the particulars of pitching. Brock's and Flood's to Pepper Martin and Frankie Frisch were about speed, spunk, and singles. Brock didn't even *have* a nickname. Flood didn't, either, although a few players on other teams called him Rembrandt, in reference to his artwork.

Curt was an artist both off the field and on. Back at McClymonds High School in Oakland—where he was a teammate of Vada Pinson, just a few years behind Frank Robinson, all of whom signed initially with Cincinnati—he produced the backgrounds for plays and big dances. He stuck with it and used his art as a release from the tensions of the big leagues, which he felt more than most players. His oil portraits were in demand, and the one he painted of Martin Luther King eventually made its way to George W. Bush.

Flood's humor and sociability were great matches for baseball, but his sensitive side was no secret to those of us who knew him well. Curt was always thinking, and that can be hazardous in our profession. As great an outfielder as he was, he said that he sometimes broke out in a sweat while waiting for a fly ball to come down. But his anxieties never left him disagreeable. The strongest reaction you'd see out of Flood was when he'd make the last out of an inning and sweep up his glove on his way to center field. On the rare days when he wasn't playing, he'd be clapping and cheering and chattering so much in the dugout that I'd tell him to go buy a ticket if he wanted to make all that noise. Curt was always witty, always fun, always making somebody smile. Often me. When I spoke at his funeral in 1997, I pointed out that he was one of the few people I knew whom I could never be mad at. Not even for an instant. And that's in spite of him being my roommate for a long time. We were constantly together on the road.

In one of the greatest trades in franchise history, the Cardinals had acquired Flood and a reserve outfielder (Joe Taylor) from the Reds after the 1957 season for three pitchers (Willard Schmidt, Marty Kutyna, and Ted Wieand) we didn't terribly miss. We were teammates in Omaha to start the 1958 season, but that didn't last long. Although he was two years younger than I was, he left me behind and spent most of the summer in St. Louis. His career, however, like mine and Brock's, took a sharp turn for the better when Johnny Keane became our manager in 1961. From that point through 1968, Curt batted .302. He arrived at the '68 Series as the only .300 hitter on either team. That year, his fourth as cocaptain with McCarver, he also won his fifth of six straight Gold Gloves. In August, he was on the cover of *Sports Illustrated,* pictured with his back to home plate, jumping into the ivy of Wrigley Field to make a spectacular catch. The caption read: "Baseball's Best Centerfielder." Willie Mays was still playing center field, if you're wondering.

As a Cardinal, Curt had excelled in just about everything but the World Series. He'd batted .200 against the Yankees in '64, .179 against the Red Sox in '67, and as he stepped in against McLain in the fifth inning, he was eager for his first postseason hit of 1968.

McLain served him a fastball on the outside corner, and Flood fouled it back.

The second pitch was a dandy sidearm slider that clipped the outside corner at the knees for strike two, looking. Harry called it a fastball. He was accustomed to broadcasting on the radio, secure in the knowledge that nobody would know the difference.

McLain was in a groove now, changing angles and locations, finding his spots, making some of his best pitches of the day. Just an inning before, I thought he'd been finished. It was more than losing his control; his demeanor appeared sluggish, lackadaisical, almost disengaged. It seemed not so much that he was beaten, but that he had lost interest. I'd obviously misread the guy. You don't win 30 games without resilience and a strong competitive spirit, to say nothing of a body that responds when you need it to.

In spite of his distractions and bad habits—fifteen gallons of Pepsi a day, for one—McLain was a horse, physically. His natural gifts were evident, but he attributed some of his endurance to a collateral effect of one of his off-season hustles. He had always bowled a lot, and done it for money, and in the winter before the '68 season he picked up the pace. Baseball had given him a reputation that he was happy to cash in on at the bowling alley, where he was indulged with continuous action through leagues and matches. Everybody wanted to beat the big-time pitcher, and not many could.

When he reported to spring training, McLain was pleased to find his legs much stronger and more durable, and surprised, he claimed—this part, I found hard to believe—that a well-conditioned lower body was such an asset to his pitching. In addition, all that hefting and rolling of the sixteen-pound ball had built up his arm, and he discovered that it no longer hurt to drop down and throw from a lower angle. He had scaled back on sidearming over the previous three or so years, and the revival of it served him extremely well. As we were seeing.

Ahead of Flood, 2-and-0, he brought an overhand fastball between the near corner and Curt's knee.

As well as Flood handled inside pitches, this one, deftly spotted, was out of his comfort zone. It was the second straight time he had popped up an inside fastball with two strikes. He hit it off the handle, into short right field, and McAuliffe backpedaled for an easy catch.

AN INNING BEFORE, Roger Maris had started our rally with a walk on four straight fastballs. McLain was no longer mired in that little funk, and this time around he caught plenty of the plate with his first pitch. It was a fastball that Roger pulled high in the air, foul.

Thankfully, I didn't hear what Harry Caray said at that point.

"It's hot," he announced, "and it's humid. Ideal baseball weather in St. Louis."

It was *typical* baseball weather in St. Louis, but *ideal*? Ideal for *whom*, Harry? A mosquito? A bird of paradise? A three-toed sloth?

John McGraw, the old-time infielder and famous manager, spent one of his forty-one seasons in St. Louis, and it was enough to make him say, "A St. Louis ball club, because of the city's summer climate wearing down the players, must be twenty-five percent stronger than any other major-league club to win."

I don't know about twenty-five percent, but I can agree that, on average, the players' postgame laundry probably weighed more at Busch Stadium than it did at other ballparks. Officially, it was eighty-three degrees on October 2, with the relative humidity as high as 71 percent. With the layers of our uniforms, the sun beating down, 54,692 fans surrounding us, and the fever of the World Series making itself felt, it was damn hot, I can tell you.

While I generally didn't mind the warmth too much, I minded it less in the early innings. We were now past that point. Our three runs in the fourth had been like a bucket of cool water on the back of my neck, but as I toasted in the dugout I was ready for another.

That was one reason to root for Roger as he dug in against McLain with two outs. Another was that he was such a good guy at the end of such a great career. I wouldn't go so far as to say that we wanted to win the World Series for *his* sake, as the best kind of farewell, but it would be a hell of a bonus.

Maris, like me, was a long-sleeves guy, and he had dealt with all kinds of heat in his time, but that didn't help him with the slider McLain now broke onto the inside corner at the knees.

What helped was that the ball didn't bounce up into Cash's glove as he bent down to pick it up. It rolled through his ankles, the Tigers' third error of the game but the first to put a runner on base.

MCLAIN'S 84TH PITCH was a fastball that Cepeda, still looking slow—John McGraw might blame the St. Louis weather, and he might have a point—fouled off to the right side. I wished he would have kept those lighter bats.

It would be no surprise if McLain were gone from the game after the next out. He was down three runs, he was working his 341st inning, the Tigers probably hoped to get two more starts out of him, and Eddie Mathews had been ready to bat for him in the top of the fifth. All that said, *I* sure wouldn't have expected to give up the ball in that situation, and I doubt that Red would have asked me to. I hadn't pitched fewer than eight innings in a game since the middle of April, my second start of the season. Over the next thirty-two, I'd averaged more than nine innings, and that includes three games when the other team didn't have to bat in the ninth.

McLain seemed to sense that, in spite of his workload, the rigors of the day, and his imminent departure, he could still get a fastball past Cha Cha; especially a *high* fastball. It probably benefited him to know that he wouldn't be required to throw many more. Whether he knew it or not, it almost certainly benefited him that Cepeda, whose swing was long and time-consuming to start with, had a history of tapering off as seasons wore on. Over his career, his batting and slugging averages were lower in September than any other month of the regular season. Playing for the Giants in the 1962 World Series, he had batted .158

against the Yankees with no home runs. Playing for us in the 1967 World Series, he had batted .103 against the Red Sox with no home runs. Of course, we believed in him anyway.

The second pitch was a bit *too* high. Orlando—who, favoring range of motion over perspiration, had cut off the left sleeve of his undershirt to the length of his jersey sleeve—let it pass for ball one.

The third wasn't quite high enough, and Cepeda ripped into it, launching a missile that cleared the left-field wall about thirty feet on the wrong side of the foul pole. It slammed against the shatterproof glass that protected the well-dressed, well-fed patrons of the Stadium Club, which hung from the upper deck.

The loud foul carried with it all sorts of complexities. It showed that, even in October, Cepeda was capable of turning on a fastball and punishing it; but it didn't necessarily mean that he could match its speed consistently. Maybe he guessed right. Maybe he read it right. Maybe he geared up for it. Maybe McLain, pitching from the stretch, had come up lacking in velocity. On the other hand, maybe Orlando's bat had looked slow earlier because he was expecting a breaking pitch or trying to guide the ball to right field. Maybe he was quicker than he'd led everybody to believe. What's more, even if a pitcher was able to figure the right answer from all of the above, there was no certainty that he could take advantage of it. If, for instance, he correctly divined that Cepeda was guessing, then maybe the guessing game was still on, and still chancy for both sides. Or maybe he guessed only on certain counts. If, however, it turned out that Cha Cha happened simply to be up to the challenge of that particular fastball in that particular spot on that particular count, maybe the next one, the same speed and movement but a couple inches higher, wider, whatever, would make him miss. It's a fluid game.

At any rate, if it were me, I wouldn't push my luck. I'd keep the next pitch away from the cleanup hitter, and put some spin on it.

So would McLain. It was a well-placed slider but just off the corner, according to Gorman. Judging by the way McLain hesitated and slumped after the call, he didn't agree.

With a 2-2 count, his next decision would be a tougher one. He wouldn't want to extend the at-bat to 3-and-2, and he wouldn't want Cepeda to let loose with the same swing he'd taken on 1-and-1.

Trusting his stuff—a large part of what made him great—McLain boldly came back with a fastball. He dropped his arm angle a bit to change the look of it, but it looked good to Cepeda nevertheless. It came in straight and fat and not especially fast.

Orlando unloaded, and the ball exploded to straightaway left field. Willie Horton, who was in the game for his bat, turned and ran sideways toward the fence, then straightened, backpedaled, reached up, and snagged the ball at the edge of the warning track. His momentum took him all the way across, and he came to a stop with his back to the wall.

	1	2	3	4	5	6	7	8	9	R	H	E
Tigers	0	0	0	0	0					0	2	3
Cardinals	0	0	0	3	0					3	3	0

(Copyright Bettmann/Corbis/AP Images)

Most Detroiters considered Al Kaline to be the second-greatest player in Tigers history, behind only Ty Cobb. At the age of thirty-three, he had already played in thirteen All-Star games, but this was his long-awaited first World Series. Kaline had missed much of the '68 season with a broken arm, and to clear room for him in the Series lineup, manager Mayo Smith made the daring decision to move Gold Glove center fielder Mickey Stanley to shortstop.

Sixth Inning

IT WASN'T MATHEWS after all, which made perfect sense. They wouldn't waste his left-handed power leading off the inning. Instead, the pinch hitter for McLain was a freckle-faced utility infielder named Tommy Matchick, the key words there—other than "pinch hitter for McLain," which was a big thing but not unexpected—being "utility infielder." That term triggered a specific response. He would see fastballs.

Growing up in Pennsylvania coal country, Matchick's favorite player as a kid had in fact been the former Yankee shortstop Tony Kubek, who on this day was roaming the stands for NBC, conducting between-innings interviews with Sinatra, Musial, Casey Stengel, various dignitaries, and my wife and daughter. Turning down a basketball scholarship, Matchick had originally signed with the Cardinals; but due to a peculiar rule in place at the time, he played in the organization for just one season. For a brief period in the late fifties and early sixties, baseball operated a First-Year Player Draft by which clubs were able to select rookie minor leaguers from other teams for as little as $8,000, and in that way the Tigers purchased Matchick after the 1962 season, when he'd just turned nineteen. Around the same time, as a by-product of the same system, they snatched Denny McLain on waivers from the White Sox.

In '68, his rookie year, Matchick had been an effective pinch hitter and also started more than a third of Detroit's games at shortstop. Being a Tiger—it seemed to come with the territory—he had demonstrated a talent for the dramatic stroke, most notably in a mid-July game against the Baltimore Orioles, the Tigers' principal challengers for the American League pennant. Detroit trailed 4–0, and didn't have a hit, when McAuliffe smacked a two-run homer in the sixth inning, and still trailed 4–3 when Matchick, a left-handed batter, did the same with two outs in the bottom of the ninth, sending a pitch from Moe Drabowsky into the overhanging upper deck at Tiger Stadium.

Needless to say, that was the furthest thing from my mind when my first fastball stayed up and away.

The second one rode in on his hands. Matchick, choking up on the bat, fouled it straight back.

In spite of his big blow against Baltimore, Matchick, like most utility infielders, was not much of a home run threat, which was the main reason for feeding him fastballs. Another, though, was the combination of the heat and the stage of the game. I'd thrown 74 pitches, and although none of the first five innings would be described as unusually taxing or stressful—other than being the first five in the World Series, against the best lineup in the American League—we were reaching the point when I'd have to keep a close watch on my breaking stuff to make sure that fatigue wasn't flattening it out.

But my fastball still felt pretty good, and I thought the next one *looked* pretty good, at the bottom of Matchick's knees or the top of his socks, either one. Gorman went with the socks, I guess, and called it ball two. I turned toward the outfield and took a moment. I wasn't really upset with myself, and wasn't really upset with the ump, but I was definitely upset at falling behind Tommy Matchick with nobody out.

The next pitch was to Gorman's liking but not Matchick's, a fastball on the outside corner for called strike two.

Although I was considered a strikeout pitcher, and had just led the National League in strikeouts (McLain had a few more than I did, and Sam McDowell of Cleveland topped all of base-ball), and would finish my career second all-time to Walter Johnson in strikeouts (Johnson had retired in 1927, but another dozen guys have since passed me, led of course by Nolan Ryan, with Steve Carlton fourth), for the most part I didn't consciously seek them out until I had two strikes on a batter. There were exceptions to that. When a pitcher came to the plate, the strikeout was definitely on the table because it was such a distinct possibility; there were certain situations, usually involving a runner on third base with less than two outs, when a strikeout was clearly called for; and there were games when the fastball was jumping and the slider was juking and they were both going right where they were supposed to go—this was shaping up as one of those—and yeah, in those games I might be a little more attuned to striking people out than I customarily was. But my general MO was that I had to get to two strikes before I could think about the third.

In that spirit, my favorite two-strike fastball was the high four-seamer, which is what Matchick saw now. Swinging late, he lifted it foul behind the Tigers' dugout.

That deserved another. He popped it straight back.

He was gradually catching up with it. Rather than switch to a curve or slider, though, I rotated the ball a quarter turn for a two-seamer, which meant it was coming down and seeking the outside corner again. I thought I hit my spot, but Gorman's right hand remained at his side. That was the cue for McCarver and me to go into our not-so-subtle pantomime of discontent. He froze for a moment, then stood up, dropped his head, and stepped across the plate before looping the ball back to me. I walked forward a few steps and waited sullenly to take the throw. Tim then turned around and quietly articulated his opinion to Gorman before turning back, smoothing some dirt that didn't need it, lowering into his squat, and setting a knee-high target for another two-seamer.

The ball arrived once more at the top of Matchick's dark blue stirrup socks, and this time he tapped it to Cepeda, who charged it, gloved it, and underhanded it softly to me as I covered first base for the sixteenth out.

THE WAY MCAULIFFE stood practically facing me at the plate, his hands next to his helmet, wrapped around the handle of a bat that he brandished vertically, at the ready in defense of the batter's box and, it seemed, the honor of the king, I wasn't sure whether to spot the fastball or run him through with a sword.

Medieval as it looked, it was a stance that he'd found expedient. In his first year of professional ball, weighing 140 pounds coming out of a small town in central Connecticut—after taking a year off high school to help restore houses in the wake of a damaging flood—he'd been overpowered by low-minors pitching. A batting coach suggested that he open his hips to get his bat around quicker. When he did that, he was able to pull the ball to right field and hold his own.

It put him on track to reach Detroit at the age of twenty and win the Tigers' starting shortstop job in 1963, at twenty-three. The next year, he played 162 games at short and produced 24 home runs, a team record for that position. The year after that marked his first of three straight All-Star appearances, the last of them coming after he'd moved across the bag to second base.

McAuliffe, whose weight leveled out at about 175 pounds, had never batted as high as .275, but in 1967 his rate of reaching base had prospered from 105 walks. In '68, he'd led the American League in runs scored. He was also a solid infielder, and although it was really no business of mine, I had to wonder why, instead of bringing Stanley in from center field to play shortstop in the Series, the Tigers didn't consider (as far as I knew) moving McAuliffe back to the position where he'd been a four-year starter and two-time All-Star. Second base, it seemed, would have been a more manageable spot for Stanley to take over on short notice, no matter how good an athlete he was. I suppose they didn't want to monkey around with two key positions at once—or three, counting center field.

Besides that, McAuliffe's role on the Tigers was clearly defined. He was not only their leadoff batter, but in all ways their instigator. His tough-mindedness was complemented by a physical capability that enabled him, in spite of his size, to play fullback on his high school football team. But his competitive makeup might have come, at least in part, from his high school baseball coach, who would promptly pull a guy off the field if he didn't run out a ground ball or meet the team standard for playing the game the right way. The Tigers were a club of hard-nosed ballplayers, and McAuliffe carried the banner. In 1969, he played half the season with torn knee cartilage so troublesome that his wife had to help him out of bed in the morning.

My success so far against Detroit was connected to keeping McAuliffe off the bases. That ended when I threw a first-pitch fastball that caught too much plate and he rapped a ground single into right field, splitting the difference between Javier and Cepeda.

POETICALLY, I GUESS, in 1968 Mickey Stanley won his first of three straight Gold Gloves—four altogether—as a center fielder. He later said that he would have enjoyed the World Series much more if he'd played it from his regular position. No matter how well he acquitted himself at shortstop, he was still an outfielder at heart. In that spirit, Stanley had done his homework before the Series and alerted Kaline, Northrup, and Horton that Lou Brock's exceptional speed had made him perhaps a bit overconfident when he ran from, say, second to home on a single, and as a result he rarely saw fit to slide.

Like Horton, Northrup, and Freehan, Stanley was a Michigander, growing up a Tigers fan in Grand Rapids, where his father drove a bakery truck at night. Ironically, the player he most admired in those days was Harvey Kuenn, a batting champion and eight-time All-Star who played four seasons of shortstop for the Tigers and then moved to center field. Kuenn would remain eight years in Detroit before being traded to Cleveland for Rocky Colavito; Stanley fifteen, his entire career.

The Michigan natives were all Tigers together for eleven seasons, and Stanley and Horton spent nearly their entire Detroit careers alongside each other, not to mention the three additional years they overlapped in the minors. The two of them were close friends, and Stanley was considered to be a soothing influence on Horton, although it wasn't always smooth sailing. There was an occasion in Puerto Rican winter ball when Stanley tried to step between Horton and an opposing player as they confronted each other. Horton, irritated by the interference, picked his buddy up by the waist and carried him off the playing field. There was another, in spring training, when Horton headed toward a fan in the stands who'd been giving him a hard time. McLain jumped on his back, and when that didn't slow Willie down, Stanley grabbed his arm. Horton simply tossed him onto the turf. None of that should imply, though, that Stanley was incapable of doling out some punishment himself. He once destroyed a bat rack for standing idly by as he popped up.

His last time at bat, I'd had success against Stanley by starting him inside and then working the outside corner. That was my basic boilerplate, and I turned to it again, slipping in a called strike on an inner-half fastball at the knees.

The slider was next; and it was perfect, if you don't mind my saying so. It stayed on the outside corner until the last moment, then veered away as Stanley started to swing and held up. No matter. Strike two called.

The great thing about an 0-2 count is the variety of options it affords, given the luxury of being choosy about location. The high fastball was a time-tested strikeout choice. The low fastball had similar possibilities, with the added potential, in this situation, to induce a double play that would end the inning. The previous pitch had nominated the slider as a candidate for strike three, and it could be rolled to an infielder just about as easily. I probably picked up more strikeouts on the slider than the fastball, because if a pitcher is known to have a good fastball, hitters gear up for it. They're a very proud species and don't want you to blow a fastball by them. That said, though, Stanley, having been flummoxed by the last slider, was fairly likely to be setting himself for another one.

I went with the two-seamer away, hoping Maxvill or Javier, and preferably both, would become involved.

Stanley bailed, reached, and missed badly, the 10th strikeout of the afternoon. Oh well.

FOR YEARS MY wife, Wendy, and I—we've been together since I retired as a player—would drive our motor home from Omaha to Cooperstown for the Hall of Fame induction week-end in July. Bill White, when he was president of the National League, would be there, too, with his wife and motor home, which I'd talked him into buying. On Saturday night, while most everybody else was attending the lavish banquet before the Sun-day main event, we'd camp nearby and enjoy our own private cookout. That was when I got to really know Sandy Koufax. Like me, Sandy's not especially keen on big crowds and small talk, and he was also miffed that, while the Hall of Fame welcomed wives to the various functions of the weekend, it didn't permit him to bring along his lady friend. So he was happy to drive her out to our little corner of the campground, where we all shared some wine, talked about wine, found something or somebody to pleasantly criticize, and generally soaked in the sociability of a quieter setting. As much as we'd crossed each other's paths as 20-game winners in the National League, and as hot a rivalry as the Cardinals and Dodgers carried on in the sixties, Sandy and I never really conversed in those days, which of course puts him in the vast majority of my opponents, and probably me in his; and yet, half a century later, we're great friends with no short-age of topics, baseball or otherwise, to kick around. I don't think either one of us ever saw that coming.

More recently I've flown most of the way to Cooperstown, and frequently, on my connections to Albany, I've found myself in the good company of Al Kaline. From there, it's another seventy miles by car, and Kaline and I have often ended up riding together. Although his entry into baseball was much quicker and smoother than mine, and his reputation as a gentleman outfielder was nothing like mine as a snarling pitcher, I knew we shared a love and talent for basketball, were roughly the same age, had both devoted all of our playing years to a single organization, and had both come out of modest beginnings in urban settings. Even so, I was surprised to learn that our common ground ran even deeper than that. Al has a son about the same age as my and Wendy's son, Chris, and in the car one day he was talking about the challenges he's faced as a father who's also a famous ballplayer. His son was going through the very same things that Chris was experiencing at the time, to the point that I finally interrupted him and said, "Shit, you sure that's not *my* kid?"

Of course, those sons hadn't been born in 1968, a year in which O. J. Simpson won the Heisman Trophy, hundreds of South Vietnamese civilians were killed in the My Lai Massacre, hippies were joined by Yippies, Tommie Smith and John Carlos raised their right fists in Mexico City while the national anthem was played during their Olympic medal ceremony, George Wallace carried five states in the presidential election, black supplanted Negro as a description of preference, and nobody hit my slider.

Not a *good* one, anyway. Except Al Kaline.

I'd started him with four straight sliders in his previous at-bat, and struck him out, for the second time, with a fifth. None of them dropped more neatly to the bottom of the knee than this one did. However, it steered clear of the corners, caught the white of the plate, and Kaline rifled it over the reach of Shannon.

Landing in the grass, the ball skipped to the left-field line, near the track, where Brock cut it off to prevent McAuliffe from scoring and limit Kaline to a double.

The Tigers hadn't put a runner in scoring position all day, and now there were two, with the middle of the order coming up. Just as troubling was the damage done to my slider.

It wasn't a premium slider, but it wasn't a clunker, either—nothing, for instance, like the one I'd hung to Stanley in the first, or the one I'd dangled to Wert in the third. That left two problematic possibilities. One, I'd reached the degree of tiredness at which I could no longer keep the slider where it needed to be against hitters as good as most of Detroit's. And two, unlike the Red Sox the year before, it had finally dawned on the Tigers—at least one of them, and the one whose lead was most likely to be followed—that I wasn't all fastball. They'd begun to look for something else.

Or maybe it was just a Hall of Fame hitter getting a really good swing at a pretty good pitch.

At any rate, it was a predicament that I'd have to resolve with Norm Cash.

IN 1976, MY first year out of the game, I teamed up on the broadcasts of *Monday Night Baseball* with Al Michaels, in his first gig for ABC, and Norm Cash, who was in his second year out of the game. The arrangement lasted only a season, but Cash was an easy guy to make friends with. As far as that goes, I find it hard not to like a man who plays the ukulele, auctions hogs, and doesn't take himself too seriously. I was aware, of course, that Norm's alcohol consumption was legendary—Whitey Herzog once had the privilege of rooming with him briefly, and said it was like having his own private accommodations—and it was obvious that he'd had come a long way from the Texas town of twenty-five people where he had driven a tractor through the cotton fields at the age of ten. If he still had a party side, though, I never witnessed it. On the other hand, I did see his domestic side. After a game we called in Detroit, Norm invited Wendy and me to join him and his wife at their house not too far away on a little lake, where we enjoyed a peaceful day on the boat he kept at his private dock.

It threw me for a loop, ten years later, to hear that Cash had drowned in Lake Michigan, just off Beaver Island, between Michigan's lower and upper peninsulas. It was after dinner and drinks, close to midnight, it had been raining, and he walked out on the dock in cowboy boots to check on his cabin cruiser. At some point, he slipped, hit his head and fell into the water. They found him in the morning, floating.

But I harbored no personal feelings for Norm when, with two on and two out in the top of the sixth, McCarver lumbered out to chat with me; and it wouldn't have mattered if I had. There was a situation at hand, and I was eager to attend to it. Figuring I could use a minute to catch my breath, however—even the bill of my cap was sweating—I allowed Tim to walk all the way to the top of the mound without snapping at him. That was actually a big step, a sign of our comfort level with each other and of my mellowing over the years. My natural tendency was to work fast, and the hairier the situation, the bigger the hurry; so when Johnny Keane became our manager he told Tim to stroll out periodically and slow me down. Tim's response was, "John, if you want him to slow down, *you* go out there, because I'm not doing it." Of course, he did come out from time to time. Sheepishly. As a rule, he'd stop a few feet from the mound, take his abuse—I told him at least once that the only thing he knew about pitching was that it was hard to hit—and then head on back, his duty done. Tim has since confessed that he can't think of a single intelligent thing he ever pointed out to me in our little mid-inning visits.

I wasn't much more tolerant of visits, or advice in general, from pitching coaches. Late in my career, Barney Schultz held that position for the Cardinals. Barney was an old teammate, a reliever, and, more to the point, a knuckleballer: What the hell could he know about the way I pitched? He approached the job as though everybody on the staff was exactly the same. Wanted me to run in the outfield, for instance. Well, by that time, my knees were shot and running in the outfield only made them worse; I put in my workouts at third base. Eventually, I told Barney that the best thing he could do for me was leave me alone. Billy Muffett, who was our pitching coach in 1967 and '68, basically took that approach. He seldom told me to do much of anything other than slow down. We got along great. Muffett, in fact, was surprised at how smoothly our interactions played out, and at one point even thanked me. When I asked what he was thanking me for, he said that he'd expected me to be an asshole toward him and was grateful that I wasn't. He happened to catch me in a good year, I suppose.

McCarver and I, on the other hand, had enough history together that I *could* be an asshole, and if I happened to exercise that particular option, Tim knew better than to be insulted; it was just me being me. It's not true, though, that he never told me anything on the mound worth saying. He might, for example, remind me that a certain batter liked to hit cripples on 2-and-0. That was useful information that I might have needed to hear, and I wouldn't be too upset about having my rhythm broken on 2-and-0. Of course, I might have given him a hard time anyway. Just because.

In this case, however, I received him patiently and heard him out. We were in full agreement—it was patently obvious—that Cash was a key hitter in the ball game, and agreed also that, left-handed or not, cleanup man or not, we needed to go after him. If I pitched him carefully and walked him, we'd still have a chance to get out of the inning with the bases loaded and Willie Horton, a right-handed batter, at the plate; but that, while a reasonable approach, wasn't my style or McCarver's either. If four balls happened accidentally, so be it; the Tigers would still be ninety feet away from their first run. But the agreed-upon plan, confirmed in an actual two-way conversation, was to throw from the windup and end this damn inning *now*.

A four-seamer, middle-in. A big swing—the kind that could tie the game in style—and a big miss.

Back in 1961, Cash had been the first player to knock a ball completely over the roof of Tiger Stadium. He'd done it again later that season, and nailed a tow truck. Of greater concern, though, was the fact that he was the only guy in the American League to reach at least 20 home runs every year since then, which spoke to the consistent threat that his power posed. He would finish second only to Kaline in career home runs as a Tiger, a pretty decent return on a player whom Detroit picked up in a 1960 trade with Cleveland for Steve Demeter, who never had another hit. It was the second time Cash had been swapped in a period of four months. Coming up with the White Sox, who went to the World Series in 1959, he was a prospect of so little regard that he scarcely played behind thirty-five-year-old Earl Torgeson, who, as Chicago's starting first baseman, batted all of .220. He never appeared in a game for the Indians. When Cleve-

land's general manager had offered Cash in exchange for Demeter, his Tigers counterpart, Rick Ferrell, was said to have
wondered whether he meant cold cash or Norm.

While Cash's long-ball potential put our three-run lead in
jeopardy, the peskier problem was that, with runners at second
and third, even a bloop single would loosen our grip on the game.
And Cash had been producing base hits at a lively rate. After
slumping in the first half of the '68 season, he had batted .333
since late July. As he dug in with his slightly open stance, eye
black smeared across both sides of his face, my future broadcasting partner represented a formidable threat on multiple fronts.

Fastball, low and inside. One-and-one.

Cash had now seen enough of that part of the plate. Mc-
Carver asked for a backdoor breaking ball, and while Kaline's
double had made me question whether I was too tired to trust
one of those, it had also provided a rush of energy that served as
the answer. This one might have been my best pitch of the day,
off-speed and nipping at the corner. Cash let it pass and Gorman
signaled strike two.

A pitcher's rhythm, of itself, is not infallible, and it's not available on demand, but when it kicks in—as it seemed to be doing
now, just when I needed it the most—he can feel it, follow it,
feed off it. It's a sensation of complete control from the moment
the motion begins, the body's promise that everything is in perfect order: the timing, the velocity, the rotation, the command,
all of it. With that assurance, a pitcher can free his mind, drop
his inhibitions, and let everything just come naturally, almost au-
tomatically. He can put his faith in what he feels so strongly and
ride its surge. For me, the rhythm rocked on for most of 1968.
In, out, high, low, rising, sinking, hardly thinking.

McCarver had a significant part in that. Tim understood

rhythm. In my case, he respected the fact that, when I had a good one going, I preferred to maintain a snappy tempo and didn't need anything or anybody screwing with it. I'd tell him to just put down the first sign he thought of, and he was happy to indulge me. We were in sync: fingers down . . . feel it and fire . . . ball back . . . fingers down . . . feel it and fire. Some catchers may have been offended if they'd been asked to just throw down a finger, maybe two, without careful consideration first, without a chance to tap into their vast knowledge of the guy at the plate. To McCarver's credit, though, he was not hard-headed—a *large* head, yes, but not an excessively hard one. He didn't stomp around and show me up if I shook him off, and in turn, extending him the same respect and courtesy, I rarely shook him off. We were in it together. And because we were so single-minded, I was able to throw the ball with conviction.

We didn't use that word at the time, but in recent years Tim and I have talked quite a bit about the power of pitching with conviction—what it means, what it leads to. Pitching with convic-tion is trusting the call because you trust yourself, your catcher, and most of all your stuff, which you throw with confidence because you know it's good enough and you know that, when it gets where it's going, it will be where it's supposed to be and accomplish what it's supposed to accomplish. It's *believing* in your pitch. There were times when I felt the rhythm so clearly, and believed in my pitch so completely, that if I missed my spot I was genuinely surprised. *What the hell happened? Let's try that again.* When the rhythm locks in, and you feel it, the feeling it-self is inadvertent believing. It's organic conviction.

And yet, I can't really explain how it was that, three pitches after giving up a line drive double to left field, I suddenly found myself in rhythm. Maybe the visit from Tim was enough to pull it together. Maybe it was the focus demanded by the urgency of the situation. In any event, I was unquestionably under its influence. My pitching rhythm started, more often than not, on the inside corner and gravitated out, it involved fastballs and back-door breaking pitches, and it strongly resembled what was going on with Norm Cash.

Now the four-seamer, up and away. And a swing, a strikeout, the side retired with no further ado.

WE KNEW, OF course, that we hadn't seen the last of McLain. He'd pitch once more in the Series for certain, and possibly twice. For now, though, his place was taken by a tall right-hander named Pat Dobson, in his second season with the Tigers.

Dobson had progressed through the Detroit system after signing out of high school for a nice bonus, but his claim to fame—aside from being a wiz at *The New York Times* crossword puzzle—would come with Baltimore in 1971, when he, Jim Palmer, Dave McNally and Mike Cuellar made the Orioles the second team in history with four 20-game winners. Later, he was a pitching coach for the Brewers, Royals, and Orioles, a nice tribute for somebody known to speak his mind and sometimes perturb his bosses in the process. Dobson was a guy, obviously, who knew what he was doing; and he had some stuff, besides. In winter ball prior to the '68 season, he had made a splash by setting a Puerto Rican record with 21 strikeouts in a game. He'd started 10 games for the Tigers, the most impressive being a shutout at Boston in early June, and pitched 125 strong innings in all, benefiting from a new slider grip taught him by Johnny Sain, the Tigers' highly regarded pitching coach.

But it was a fastball that he first offered McCarver, who, deep in the box but crowding the plate, watched it sail significantly outside and high.

Apparently, Dobson wasn't satisfied with the feel and outcome of that pitch. After receiving the return throw from Freehan, he used the spikes on his right shoe to scrape vigorously at the dirt in front of the rubber. To a reliever, following pitchers who've made their own ruts and depressions where they push off and come down, the contours of the mound can present a challenge. The footing at the edge of the rubber is the contact point where a guy sets his foundation and gathers his moving parts. I usually started on the right side, but I'd occasionally scoot over to the left against a left-handed hitter. Either way, I'd drag my right foot so violently after my delivery that the joint in my big toe would swell up, skin would scrape off, and my sock would soak up blood. The dragging would also leave a large hole by the rubber, and that could be bothersome to the opposing pitcher if he drove off from the same spot. The landing area can be an issue, as well. It's the terminal for all the thrust a pitcher generates, and any irregularity there, created by the touch-downs of somebody else, can turn an ankle or, short of that, bring about a tentativeness that throws everything off. A pitcher coming out of the bullpen has to make sure that the mound is fit to work from, and to a lesser extent the same considerations apply to starting pitchers when they return, every inning, to surfaces that their opponents have customized. McLain and I were good with the groundskeeping, but Dobson was dealing with foreign soil and looked to be uncomfortable on it. Hey, Tim, take another one!

Guess he couldn't hear me. Dobson's next pitch—either a sinking fastball or the slider that Sain had taught him—arrived at the knees, on the outer half, and McCarver couldn't resist. He sand-wedged it to McAuliffe, who backed up and collected it in short right field.

THE MORE I think about it, and watch the video, the more surprised I am to see Shannon choked up on the bat, like a Punch-and-Judy hitter. He doesn't look like one and certainly doesn't *sound* like one; not these days, anyway, when we're sitting around telling tales. Mike seems to remember every home run he ever hit, and greatly enjoys sharing those recollections, to the point that I've sympathized with him about Hank Aaron sneaking past to break his record by a mere 687. I can only imagine the stories he tells his eighteen grandchildren.

But the Moon Man *was* a burly guy, and he *was* a power hitter—at least, by Cardinal standards—and over the subsequent decades, through his visibility and regaling, he has become a fine ambassador for the ball club; that is, for both the organization and our particular club, as constituted in the sixties. His status as a St. Louis broadcasting icon has provided him the public platform, and his popular restaurant, a block from the new ballpark, has become a kind of headquarters for Cardinal fans. For that reason, though, it's not a place where I can hang out, although it's well appointed and the food is excellent. Unfortunately, when an establishment is packed with that many redshirts, as I call the folks who crowd the streets around Busch Stadium, ex-Cardinals like me—or Torre or Brock or McCarver or Schoendienst or Shannon himself, guys I'd love to dine and have a drink with—become part of the entertainment. Nothing against the fans. St. Louis fans are as good as it gets. Before he retired as commissioner, Bud Selig referred to St. Louis as "the best baseball city" in the country, and I wholeheartedly agree. It's a combination of the fans and the organization. The Cardinals care about their tradition, and they care about their fans, and it's a beautiful relationship. We old guys have a role in that, which I understand and appreciate. But there's a time and place, neither of which is dinner.

Years ago, the restaurant most associated with the Cardinals was Stan Musial and Biggie's, and I rarely went there either. The first time I did, they wouldn't serve us. Curt Flood had a similar experience. But I should point out that it wasn't Stan's doing, that's for sure. He wasn't on the premises at the time, and I don't believe they even told him about it. At any rate, the players I hung out with didn't congregate at Musial's, and if there's an occasion nowadays to gather at Shannon's, it will be in the off-season and the back door will be involved, pointing us down the stairs to a room out of view. There will be wine, and distorted remembrances of the distant past, and every time we pass the bread, Shannon will knock another ball out of the park. I'll ask him how many home runs he has now, for crying out loud, and he'll be mad at me for a minute or two.

I half expected him to rip one that day against Dobson, especially after the first pitch ran in on his hands and the second, a big curveball, stayed a little high. Needing a strike, Dobson would probably throw a fastball, and given the way he was going, chances were good that the fastball would not be delivered with precision as a top priority or a likely result.

Instead it was another curveball, and worse than the last one, loopy and tantalizing and as meaty as I'd hoped a fastball would be. Shannon whaled at the thing, but he must have been thinking along the lines that I was because he was well ahead of it, pulling it foul into the seats between third base and the plate. Two-and-one.

There's not a lot of difference between a 2-0 count and 2-and-1. If the bases are loaded, in which case a walk is generally not an option, the batter can perhaps be a little more confident of seeing a strike—and maybe one with room to spare—on 2-and-0. But under normal circumstances, a pitcher might actually be more generous on 2-and-1, when he still likes his chances, because ball three would change the dynamics so dramatically in the hitter's favor.

And now came the fastball.

Again, Dobson's pitch was plump, and again Shannon pounced on it; but only Willie Mays could take advantage of every mistake that came his way. Shannon pounded the ball into the ground, sending it on a high bounce to Stanley, who stayed back on it—he probably had to—and gloved it in a mechanical kind of way that Maxvill or Ozzie Smith or any slick, everyday shortstop, including Ray Oyler, would not have. The transfer to his hand was not quicker than the eye, like Javier's, but his arm was strong and the throw was straight and Shannon, running hard—no doubt angry that the ball wasn't banging off the bleachers or at least the wall—was beaten to first by a quarter of a step.

IF JAVIER HADN'T stood so far away from the plate, the first pitch would have sailed directly over his head. And it wasn't put there on purpose. Dobson was just out of whack; and we weren't holding him accountable, damn it.

The fact was, we had only three hits, and were fortunate that two of them, the fourth-inning singles by Shannon and Hoolie, had come back-to-back after a couple of uncharacteristic walks from McLain. But even when McLain had struggled with his control, he'd shown a lot more of it than Dobson had brought out of the bullpen. And he was McLain. McLain had won more games in July alone than Dobson had won in his big-league career. We needed to take advantage of the opportunity that the Tigers were presenting us.

Fastball inside.

I hadn't minded much when Shannon let it fly on 2-and-0, because the pitch was there and Mike was a big strong guy. But I'd have preferred that Hoolie not poke at and foul off the sinking slider that Dobson now dropped at knee level, his best effort of the inning. Javier, though, was not a noted champion of the base on balls. He consistently walked around 25 times a year in everyday duty, a disinclination that, alongside his modest power and batting averages, would get him eaten alive by the critics in today's numbers game. I'm not counted among those who have come to view walking as the secret to life and getting around the bases, but I always thought that if Javier had done a little more of it, he could have taken much better advantage of his speed. He wouldn't have been Brock, but he'd have been about the nearest thing we could hope for in the bottom third of the batting order.

On this occasion, however, he had little choice but to watch Dobson's next fastball cross at his Adam's apple and the following pitch, a stray curve, droop in even higher for ball four.

I expected Hoolie to run now, as he successfully had in the fourth, but was glad he didn't on the first pitch to Maxvill. It was marginally high and outside, in a spot that would have made it convenient for Freehan to rise out of his crouch and throw to second base.

Dobson's continuing lack of control was welcomed by Maxvill, the third straight Cardinal hitter to choke up on the bat. Maxie was far more willing than Javier to let bad pitches go by, although nine of his 52 walks that year had actually been intentional, which I could never figure out. With '68 being his best-ever offensive season, he did manage to outhit all of our pitchers; but even then, Carlton nosed him out in home runs, 2–1. Dal simply wasn't a guy who could do much damage with the bat, and even with two outs—the setting, typically, in which he'd be passed on purpose—I always thought it was a mistake to walk him and bring up the pitcher. Even if the threat was successfully ended that way, we'd have the top of the order starting off the following inning. The top of our order, bear in mind, was Brock and Flood.

The second pitch to Maxie, on which Javier took off, was also outside, and higher than the first. Freehan's throw to second base arrived at the bill of Stanley's cap, and as he began to bring the ball down for the tag, Javier slid in cleanly. A moment later, Stanley's glove reached Javier's backside, and the second-base umpire, Stan Landes, called Hoolie out.

Of course, we were still a couple generations away from instant replay rules, but NBC did have instant replay *cameras*. They plainly confirmed that Pat Dobson—nine balls, four strikes, one bad call, and three official batters—had just thrown one helluva lucky inning.

	1	2	3	4	5	6	7	8	9	R	H	E
Tigers	0	0	0	0	0	0				0	4	3
Cardinals	0	0	0	3	0	0				3	3	0

(Herb Scharfman/Getty Images)

I always grumbled about our inability to score runs, but it wasn't for lack of speed or hitting skill at the top of the lineup. As far as I'm concerned, Brock (right) and Flood were the best one-two combo in the game. They finished with the same career batting averages (.293). Lou, of course, stole a lot more bases and played much longer, but Curt made history by *not* playing longer. He also won seven Gold Glove awards.

Seventh Inning

IN A GAME at Fenway Park, Willie Horton once popped a ball straight up and whacked an unsuspecting pigeon, which dropped lifeless in front of home plate. As a footnote, and I suppose a sign of how cold-blooded a hitter he was, he singled on the next pitch.

The pigeon fatality came to mind in connection with the foul ball he hit on my first delivery of the seventh inning, a four-seamer on the outer half. This one was not life-threatening, thanks to the screen behind home plate, but it was a murderous cut that Willie unleashed. Even with the heavy bat he swung, the big man could explode on a fastball.

At that point of his career—age twenty-five, his sixth of eighteen seasons—Horton was at the peak of his power, generating more home runs than he ever had or ever would again, in a year when long-ball hitting, like every other kind, was at an infamous low. Although he'd already experienced leg and ankle problems and underwent surgery after the '67 season, he hadn't yet been visibly diminished by the chronic injuries that ultimately would cause him so much distress, undermining not only his production but his status on the ball club and even his popularity in Detroit. Willie was a proud guy, and reacted emotionally when he felt unappreciated or unfairly judged. He ducked out of batting practice and refused to pose for a team picture. In '69, stuck in a wretched slump and booed by his hometown fans, he walked off the field in the middle of a game and stayed away for four days. After the final game of '71, when the club was managed by Billy Martin and the two of them had words over the running out of a ground ball, Horton, who would play in Detroit for another five years, declared that his time as a Tiger had come to an end.

Somehow, though, in spite of his little rebellions—I suspect it's because he had such a good heart—Willie was never considered a bad apple. To the contrary, when Martin was managing the Yankees in 1985, he actually hired Horton as a "harmony coach," an interesting concept for an organization whose tone was set by Martin and George Steinbrenner. Fifteen years later, the Tigers brought Willie back as a special advisor and liaison to the city's African American community, a capacity in which he remains. The team has retired his number 23 and immortalized him with a statue just behind the left-field fence at Comerica Park. The statue captures him following through on a hefty swing a lot like the one that opened the seventh inning.

It was the second time in the game that he'd led an inning off, and on both occasions he'd come out of the dugout hacking. On our previous engagement, two innings before, he'd popped up a slider that broke to the outside corner. That sounded pretty good, but this one dove into the dirt for ball one.

As impressive as Horton's rip had been on the initial fastball, I remembered our first meeting, back in the second inning, and still wasn't convinced that he could time *every* fastball, particularly one that followed a slider, in the dirt or not. I now brought a two-seamer to roughly the same spot where I'd put the pitch that he'd fouled so ferociously a few moments before.

He timed it quite well, actually. The result was a line drive a couple steps to Maxvill's right. Maxie was quick enough to cross over, reach—with both hands again—and snag the ball wide of his head for the first out.

Dobson, thankfully, had left a little of his luck on the mound.

THE BATTLES WITH Jim Northrup had been a couple of the most sharply contested of the day. They'd been waged inside and out, with no consistent pattern to the pitch selection, and both times the outcomes had been decided on sliders, first with a swinging strike and then with the same kind of line drive to Maxvill that Horton had just hammered. (When Joe Cronin, the American League president, was interviewed by Kubek, he whined a bit about the Tigers' two hardest-hit balls going right to the shortstop; but, you know, Maxie had been in that same spot for the last six months, and he hadn't missed many of those.)

It seemed to me that Northrup embraced the gamesmanship involved with what we all did for a living. It also seemed that, with him trying to figure me out and me trying to make that as difficult as possible, there would probably be some hit-and-miss, so to speak, a certain randomness—that is, a higher degree of it than might be found across the board—to the results we mutually arrived at.

He had been swinging at most of what I'd thrown him on the inner half of the plate, but this time I started him with a four-seamer deliberately *off* the inner half. Northrup began to offer at it, but stepped back and held up as the pitch whizzed under his hands.

Its purpose, of course, was to prepare the outside corner, which I now addressed with a backdoor slider. It veered closer to center than I'd intended, but the break was severe enough to discourage Northrup from swinging as the ball, traveling at about a four-o'clock angle, shot down to knee level, strike one.

The last time he'd batted, I'd strung together fastballs. This time, sliders. The next one followed the same general design as the pitch before it, breaking slightly less and benefiting from a more desirable location—from my perspective—nearer the outside corner. Once more, Northrup let it go and Gorman called the strike.

I mopped my forehead and grabbed a couple deep breaths as Northrup turned and walked slowly to the edge of the batting circle, bent his head, and stared at the dirt, no doubt thinking things through. His walk back was even slower. With all deliberation, he returned to the box, adjusted his helmet, then stepped out again with his right foot before, at last, digging in for good. It appeared to me that, when he reset himself, he might have been a little farther forward, maybe in defense of another breaking ball.

At 1-and-2, a high four-seamer would make a lot of sense here anyway. When Northrup had driven the ball to Maxvill in the fifth, it had been on a slider that broke inside; in fact, the second pitch in a row of that description. Come to think of it, having previously pummeled an inside slider in a comparable situation, he wouldn't expect *another*, would he? In that light, the high four-seamer would make a lot of sense to *him*, too. Maybe I was mistaken about where he was setting up. Probably was. He had to be thinking fastball, didn't he? Besides that, I'd fallen into a slider rhythm.

And so, the slider, breaking low and in, where I ordinarily

wouldn't put it against a good left-handed hitter. Northrup was making me improvise—more than that, to contradict my usual tendencies—in mid-battle.

And yet, he gave every indication of expecting the kind of pitch he now saw spinning his way. He geared up, snapped his right hip toward the Cardinal dugout, and whipped his bat around with conviction and force.

But there's more to guessing than pitch selection. Location, location, location. The ball was well off the plate by the time McCarver caught it.

IT WAS MY 12th strikeout, and Harry Caray took the opportunity to point out that I was now just three away from tying the single-game World Series record that Koufax had set exactly five years before, to the day, against the Yankees. I can promise you that I had no inkling of any such thing, or immediate interest in it, and I'm pretty sure nobody behind me, or in our dugout, did either. If there was an exception, which I seriously doubt, it would probably have been Roger Maris, who on October 2, 1963, had batted fifth in the Yankee lineup, four spots behind Kubek and just after Mantle. He was 0-for-4, striking out once.

Like McLain and me in '68, Koufax had won both the Cy Young and MVP awards that year. He'd also picked up his second of five straight ERA titles, a run of pitching domination that hasn't been equaled in my lifetime. He did it with a rising fastball (which, technically, doesn't actually rise but looks like it does because it doesn't descend like the batter expects it to) that he kept on the outside corner; a huge, overhand, unhittable (even though batters often knew it was coming from the way he held his hands in his windup) curveball that you could actually *hear* (the only other audible curve I knew of belonged to an old-timer named Sam Jones); long fingers with which he was able to produce an exceptionally fast rotation on the ball (which is what made his fastball jump and his curve plummet); and an arthritic elbow that ultimately prevented him from straightening his left arm and forced him to suddenly retire in 1966 at the age of thirty, having just led the National League in wins (27, his career high), ERA (1.73, his career low), innings pitched, complete games, and strikeouts. Five years later, Koufax became the youngest player ever elected to the Hall of Fame.

On the day he struck out 15 Yankees, Sandy beat the great Whitey Ford 5–2. He bested Ford again in game four, 2–1, completing the Dodgers' sweep. Koufax had been 25–5 in 1963, his first 20-win season, and after catching a glimpse of him in the Series, Yogi Berra said, "I can see how he won twenty-five games. What I don't understand is how he lost five."

Although his arm was always spectacular—and although he did strike out 18 San Francisco Giants one night during his formative years—Koufax didn't put it to its best advantage until he was twenty-five and in his seventh season with the Dodgers. Coming out of Brooklyn, he played basketball at the University of Cincinnati, where his freshman coach, Ed Jucker, also ran the baseball team. When his first basketball season ended, Sandy persuaded Jucker to come watch him throw a few in the gym, made the club, struck out a bunch of batters, walked just about as many, and signed with the Dodgers when they were still playing in his hometown. He was part of their starting rotation when they moved to Los Angeles in 1958, but his relationship with the strike zone approximated mine at a similar age. For Koufax, that changed one spring training when his catcher, Norm Sherry, who was also his roommate, convinced him to stop trying to throw so damn hard on every pitch. Following that advice, Sandy found the touch and command he would need to craft four no-hitters (three more than I did), win three Cy Youngs (one more than I), and in 1965 set a modern record for strikeouts in a season (382, later eclipsed by Nolan Ryan's 383).

He overcame his wildness shortly before I did. I know this because, when Johnny Keane became our manager during the 1961 season and took on the mission of making me believe that I could in fact get the ball over the plate, the example he used was Koufax. He pointed out that Koufax had preceded me in two respects: not only was his aim severely off, but he relied too much on his fastball.

Keane picked the perfect model, because when I saw Koufax in person he was very often shutting us out. Ten times he held the Cardinals scoreless, four more times than any other team. In 1961, he shut us out 1–0 (thanks to a seventh-inning home run by Tommy Davis on an inside fastball), and his opponent was yours truly. In 1962, he again shut us out 1–0 (thanks to a ninth-inning home run by Tommy Davis, again on an inside fastball), and his victim was once more your humble narrator. He got me in '63, as well, even without a home run from Tommy Davis, who saw no more inside fastballs.

I hated pitching against Sandy, and it wasn't because the games would be tense and leave no margin for error; that part of it I embraced. It was because he had us beaten before we took the field. At one point, Keane called a pregame meeting on a day when Sandy was pitching against us and said that anybody who tried to pull the ball against him would be fined a hundred dollars. But the problem was not trying to pull the ball. The problem—aside from his fastball and curve—was that Koufax intimidated the Cardinals, and I found that hard to swallow. If there was to be any intimidating going on from a pitcher in a game that I was involved with, I strongly preferred that pitcher to be me.

Anyway, I had no idea what the record was for strikeouts in a World Series game, and no idea who held it. But if I'd had to guess who, I'd have probably said Sandy.

FREEHAN'S SHIRT WAS dark and heavy now with seven innings of steady perspiration, and the advancing afternoon was offering little sympathy. As he dug into the right-handed batter's box, his shadow mimed him from directly behind, the sun having drifted over the first-base dugout. The giveaway straw hats were coming in handy to the men—most of them in short-sleeved white shirts, more than a few wearing ties—sitting in the left side of the stadium. Some of the spruced-up ladies modeled them also, and others battled the brightness with visors.

After some quiet early innings, the St. Louis fans were beginning to rumble again. I figured it was because we were seven outs away from taking the lead in the World Series. That was the surge I felt in my chest. Late in a tight or important ball game—hell, *any* ball game—the pursuit of winning consumed me. But Harry said it was the strikeouts causing all the commotion. Fortunately, I couldn't hear him, and barely heard the 54,000 he was referring to.

My two-seam fastball ran low and away.

I knew from exhausting experience that Freehan wouldn't make it easy early in the count. But his power discouraged me from giving in to him, especially with two outs and the bases clear. I'm no fan of the prevent defense, anyway. I don't like when my Nebraska Cornhuskers drop into it with a fourth-quarter lead, and I wasn't about to put the ball on a tee for a team with the thunder and late-inning track record of the Tigers.

A slider, my 100th pitch of the day, missed in the same vicinity as the two-seamer.

At 2-and-0, with my rhythm temporarily lapsed, I was no longer in the finger-down-and-fire mode. I stared in at McCarver and kept staring. Sometimes, I did that to shake off a sign. Other times, I was just taking a moment. Other times, *Tim* was just taking a moment.

We weren't going to make Freehan impatient, but we could perhaps use his patience to our advantage. For instance, with an edge in the count he might well be holding out for a centered fastball to drive. My only objection to throwing a slider in this scenario would be the concern about locating it properly with seventh-inning, 100-pitch fatigue; but my guess was that, putting his patience into play, he'd lay off a breaking pitch.

Which he did. The slider started at his hands, and he only flinched as it bent over the inner half of the plate for strike one called.

Quickening the pace, I wound up for a fastball as Freehan was reassuming his stance. It was a low two-seamer, outer half. He looped it back and slightly right.

Now *he* was stalling, stepping out and walking about. I was eager to throw the curveball that I could feel in my fingers.

It was a big one, with plenty of arc and a change of pace. For one of two reasons, Freehan ducked his shoulder as the ball, headed toward the inner half, dropped across the letters of his soaked jersey: he was either too taken aback to swing the bat or he trusted that Gorman would call it high. Gorman called it high. It probably was, in spite of what the 54,000 had to say.

Freehan's at-bat, the second in which he'd pushed me to a full count, had now encompassed all three pitches, the east and west sides of the plate, and the northern and southern extremities of the strike zone. And that was on top of the ten pitches he'd seen in the third inning, when he finally struck out checking his swing on a slider that caught the outside corner.

Okay, then.

This slider *started* on the outside corner, but I don't believe it stayed there. It swerved away from Freehan as he triggered his swing and then tried, in vain, to stop it. His left hip was pointed to Shannon, his hands extended toward Maxvill, his bat held aloft, when McCarver caught the ball several inches beyond the black and about that far above the dirt, setting off the seventh-inning stretch.

GIVEN THAT MAXVILL had been at the plate when Javier was officially thrown out stealing to end the sixth, there he was again to lead off the bottom of the seventh. Dobson was back, as well, picking right up where he left off.

The first pitch was a tight fastball that made Maxie take evasive action. When the next, a sinker, dropped low, the count on Dal had reached 2-and-0 for the second time in a matter of minutes.

This was shaping up nicely. In light of Maxvill's inclination to walk and Dobson's apparent generosity along those lines and the opportunity to bunt—if Dobson didn't walk me, too— that I would be happy to seize if the trend continued, and of course Brock and Flood coming up behind me . . .

I'll be damned if Maxie didn't swing at the very next pitch. It was another sinker, slightly elevated and reasonably hittable, but there was little chance that even a favorable outcome would take him beyond first base, which was only two balls—Dobson's specialty of the day—away. This, however, was an unfavorable outcome. A pop-up. Cash trotted halfway down the first-base line to catch it in foul territory.

Just for the record, I'll point out that two of the next three pitches were, indeed, balls. To the pitcher. The exception was the first, an inviting curve that I took a rip at and fouled back.

The next was a floating breaking pitch in the neighborhood of my helmet. I ducked and we moved on. Dobson's wildness, along with his pitch selection, made it pretty clear that he hadn't been throwing at me. If he had been, it's not likely that the ball would have ventured that close. He simply had no idea where it was going when it left his hand.

Fastball, high.

Now, if I were sitting in the dugout watching me bat, or if I were writing about it forty-seven years after the fact, I'd have to advocate taking another pitch in this scenario. I mean, if I'm going to second-guess Maxvill for helping out an opposing pitcher who was grappling with obvious command issues, it's my obligation, I suppose, to contend that a swing would be inadvisable here, also—same pitcher, still grappling—even if Dobson had already thrown me a strike.

It was a fastball on the outside corner at the belt. I didn't even get that good of a whack at it. My front foot went the wrong way and I'll be damned if I, too, didn't serve the ball in the air to Cash—essentially the same harmless pop-up that Maxvill had just gotten himself out with, only on the other side of the baseline.

ON OUR CLUB, nobody was sacred. Nobody was exempt from the prick of the needle. But Lou Brock was about the closest thing.

It's not that he was a forbidding person or an unimpeachable player. Some of us questioned it when he stole third base with two outs and a five-run lead. He was known to throw a ball into the tenth row of the stands now and then. And when he went to pick up a grounder in the outfield, he did so with what I called floppy hands. As a rule, though, Lou didn't comport himself as one whom our twisted clubhouse humor could easily cut down to size. But there were ways. One of the important responsibilities I took on for the ball club was a pregame quiz, sort of like Cardinal Charades, in which I'd present unflattering imitations of various teammates and they'd have to identify who I was. The tradition was started and perfected by a backup catcher named Dave Ricketts, our best agitator, but any of us might jump in when somebody had done some unfortunate thing in a ball game—usually the previous night's—that we simply couldn't allow to pass. Brock was a bit of a challenge, but I could get everybody to shout out his name if I put a glove on my right hand, had somebody roll out a ball, and clumsily flicked at it. Floppy hands.

Another of my solemn duties was an annual end-of-season evaluation of everybody's chances to be back with the club the following spring. I'd put the names on a blackboard and methodically cross them out, one by one—perhaps with a sensitive explanation of their shortcomings ("McCarver, you never *could* throw")—until, year after year, the only names left were Gibson and Brock. (Once, I included and crossed out our general manager, Bing Devine, and the guys seemed to get an unusually big kick out of that. I hadn't realized that Bing was standing right behind me.)

But Brock really was a marvel. The man set a record by stealing 118 bases *when he was thirty-five*! It was my next-to-last season, and as much as my knees hurt at that point, I was glad to be around for it. Lou played until he was forty, when he batted .304—along the way picking up his 3,000th hit—before retiring as the career leader in steals. That was 1979, which happened to be the rookie season for Rickey Henderson, who would break both of Lou's major records. A lot of people consider Henderson to be the greatest leadoff batter of modern times, and I don't begrudge him that distinction; but I'm a Brock man, floppy hands and all.

And I truly expected him to take Pat Dobson out of the park, if he ever got a pitch to hit.

Dobson started him off with a nasty sinker at the knees, outside corner, called strike, his best pitch of the day. Brock seemed confident that the Tigers' reliever couldn't throw three of those. He rearranged some dirt under his feet but never left the batter's box, locking into his closed stance as Dobson picked up the rosin bag and dropped it back down to his right. A curveball passed by, high.

Even with two outs and nobody on, an inning remained very much alive with Brock at the plate. A single or walk put him virtually at second base. What's more, in '68 his doubles and triples had carried him into scoring position another sixty times. And while his home run output had fallen off that year, his raw power had not.

Except that now, as he awaited the 1-1 pitch, Lou lightly swung his right arm around, suggesting that he might still be bothered by the shoulder he'd fallen on while helping himself to second base in the third inning. Then again, he played hurt all the time. He had to, with all that sliding on steals and diving back from leadoffs and getting hit by pitchers who didn't look kindly upon the steals and leadoffs.

Dobson spun a curve to the knees, and Lou tapped it foul to the left.

With two strikes, it seemed curious that Wert, the third baseman, was still positioned in close, at the cutout of the grass, in defense of a bunt down the line. Brock would not be bunting that way or any other.

He bent backward as a high fastball blew past the two redbirds perched on the bat across his chest.

A low fastball filled out the count.

And now Brock's speed enhanced his power. A pitcher didn't want the aggravation of walking him. Not *him*. This is your pitch, Lou!

Dobson chose a curve, and it broke to the bottom of the strike zone, center of the plate, much to my man's liking. Lou approached the ball with certainty, squared it properly, and watched it rise toward the shadows in right-center field, where it settled three rows beyond the fence, more than four hundred feet from where he had just limbered his shoulder and worked the count full.

It was Brock's third World Series, and the great base stealer had now homered in every one.

FLOOD, HAVING SET himself as close as he could to home plate, his feet spread wide apart, had to step out of the box as Dobson backed off the rubber and turned toward the outfield, chomping on his chewing gum. A neatly dressed usher in a flat-topped, white-billed hat was collecting the toilet paper that one of our enthusiasts had flung in the vicinity of Northrup.

I couldn't have imagined that this would be Curt's last happy year as a Cardinal. He was essential to who we were and especially important to me, a teammate I could both enjoy and admire. He was clever, thoughtful, well-read, interesting—an ideal roommate, except for his smoking. (I hadn't smoked since the day when I was thirteen and slipped into a closet at home to light up on the sly. My older brother Josh, who was also my coach and role model, found me out, opened the door, and popped me in the head. So much for that. I was just grateful that he didn't turn me over to our mother.)

Otherwise, Curt and I were in sync, the kind of friends who could tolerate each other's eccentricities—he hardly ever complained when I screamed at the television after losing a game—and communicate with a glance or a nod or even less. One Sunday morning, as we were about to leave the room for a ball game, the TV was turned to an evangelist, who urged everybody to put their hands on the set if they were believers. Without saying a word or even looking at each other, we both walked up, placed our hands on the television, and continued on out the door. Another time, we were having lunch at a coffee shop in Philadelphia, and I was wearing my sunglasses. Curt, who never missed a thing, whispered that the guys in the next booth thought I was Ray Charles. When we were finished eating, I fumbled around for my wallet, Curt grabbed my arm to lead me out, and one of the Ray Charles fans said, "See, I told you!" Unfortunately, after a few years of rooming with Curt, his smoking bothered me to the extent that I asked the club for separate accommodations, which of course I had to pay for.

But we remained close, even as 1969 got off to a rough start for both of us. I was serving temporarily as the Cardinals' representative to the Players Association, and in that role appeared during spring training on *The Tonight Show*, where Johnny Carson asked me about the possibility of an imminent strike. The union was becoming more proactive under the new leadership of Marvin Miller, focusing in particular on the owners' attempt to reduce the players' percentage of television revenue after MLB had signed a hefty network contract. I raised that point on the show, and one of the owners who didn't fully appreciate it was ours, August Busch.

It wasn't lost on Mr. Busch that I had just received a nice salary increase. When I got back to St. Petersburg, he called a team meeting and invited reporters to sit in, which was highly unusual. He had something to say, and wanted it publicly known. The gist of his message was that the players were making plenty of money, we ought to have been grateful for that rather than greedy for more, and it was incumbent upon us to not alienate the fans or front office. What we heard, basically, was shut up and play ball. He handed copies of his speech to the press.

While my contract—the highest on the team at $125,000—was nothing to complain about, Flood was less satisfied with his. Following a season in which he'd won another Gold Glove, made the All-Star team, finished fourth in the MVP voting, and led the club in hitting, the Cardinals had offered him just a moderate raise to a figure that didn't approach the $90,000 he had in mind. He threatened to not play under those terms; and when the impasse reached the media, strained relations were only aggravated. Making it worse for Curt, his brother, who had been living with him in St. Louis while on parole, attempted to rob a jewelry store around this time. The situation escalated with hostages, a commandeered police car, a chase down city streets, and television coverage.

Then, a few days after Busch's ominous meeting, Cepeda was traded. The sudden move wasn't perceived by the players as retribution, necessarily, for anything Orlando had done—and we didn't question that it was a fair baseball exchange, with Joe Torre coming our way—but it *was* a signal that management cared little about the special atmosphere we'd created, or even the special things we'd accomplished. The scene had changed. Adios, El Birdos.

I'm sure that Curt felt all this even more than most of us did. Even without the contract dispute, or the family troubles, he'd have felt it more than most of us. He wasn't the type to let shifting winds just blow on by. Many times, in our hotel room, I'd seen him sitting on the edge of the bed, smoking a cigarette, lost in thought.

And yet, he wasn't the type to mope, carry anger with him, or impose his feelings on other people. As much as he suffered in 1969, he never made his *teammates* suffer. On the surface, he seemed like the same Curt. Although the club struggled— it was the first season of divisional play, and we finished in a disappointing fourth place, 13 games behind the Mets—and Flood's batting average dropped below .300 for only the second time in seven years, he otherwise performed to his customary standard. And as usual, he made me feel good when he was around.

But he wouldn't be around anymore.

Less than a week after our season ended, the Cardinals traded Curt, McCarver, Joe Hoerner, and a reserve outfielder named Byron Browne to the Phillies for Dick Allen—I didn't mind that at all—Jerry Johnson, and Cookie Rojas. It's worth noting that McCarver had replaced me as player rep. It's also worth noting that, somewhere in all of this, I was removed from consideration for an Anheuser-Busch distributorship.

My main problem with the trade was that we were losing two great ballplayers who happened to be my best friends on the team. Curt's main problem was having his life uprooted without a say in it.

He had an art studio and a nightclub in St. Louis. He had friends and history there. And having grown up in Northern California, sensitive to his rebellious surroundings . . . having strong convictions about personal rights . . . having a deep-seated, unshakable sense of principle . . . he would not report to Philadelphia. He would not accept the trade.

Of course, baseball's reserve clause—a product of its anti-trust exemption—allowed for nothing of the sort. Knowing that the only alternative was to challenge the reserve clause in court, Curt contacted Marvin Miller, who told him that a legal appeal would be very expensive and time-consuming. Economically, it was a losing proposition. To Curt, though, that was a minor point. He believed the prevailing system was unfair and fundamentally wrong, and he simply wasn't going to stand for it anymore.

And he was right; it was wrong. I agreed, and told him so. I said, "I'm behind you a hundred percent . . . but about thirty steps back." He laughed, but it was actually a pretty fair description of where I stood. I was not as idealistic as Curt, and too pragmatic to consider doing what he was doing; less urgently motivated, for sure. I hadn't read James Baldwin or Ralph Ellison as avidly as he had. I hadn't protested in Mississippi with Martin Luther King and Jackie Robinson, as he had. I hadn't been traded or disrespected in contract negotiations. But I sympathized with his repudiation of the plantation culture that seemed to guide baseball's treatment of its players.

Here's one small example that brought it home for me: In 1959, when I needed a GPS to find home plate but it hadn't been invented, the Cardinals sent me back to the minors when we were nearing the end of a road trip. Our meal money was ten dollars a day, and the traveling secretary figured that I should have thirty dollars left of it. The plane ticket to Omaha was twenty-seven dollars, so he told me to just buy it with the rest of my meal money. But I'd spent a few bucks in Cincinnati and didn't have enough. So they bought me the ticket and took it out of my paycheck. Technically, the club had the right to do that, but it was the kind of petty little thing that exemplified the player-owner relationship. And it was the kind of thing that Curt was just tired of. The trade brought it all to a boil.

On the day before Christmas, he submitted a letter to the commissioner, Bowie Kuhn. "I do not feel that I am a piece of property to be bought and sold irrespective of my wishes," he wrote. ". . . I, therefore, request that you make known to all Major League clubs my feelings in this matter, and advise them of my availability for the 1970 season." When Kuhn, as expected, denied his request, Curt sued.

The trial began in May. In August, the federal court ruled in favor of Major League Baseball. Curt took the case to the U.S. Court of Appeals, which in 1971 also sided with the owners. Curt then appealed to the Supreme Court, which in 1972 upheld the reserve clause by a vote of five to three.

Meanwhile, after sitting out a year, Flood signed with the Washington Senators in 1971—for considerably more money than he'd requested from the Cardinals two years earlier—but played in only thirteen games. His heart wasn't in it. The ordeal and alcohol had stripped him of his drive. There were also death threats. (Of course, you didn't have to sue baseball to sample the hostility of hateful fans. Especially if you were black. Setting records was a good way to do it, as well. Brock received threats. Hank Aaron was inundated by them. And I fielded my share, many of which followed this particular World Series.)

Needing to get away, Curt moved to Europe, living at various times in Copenhagen, Majorca—where he operated a tavern until it was closed down by the police—and Andorra. He partied, drove a Porsche, knew women, ran up his debt, and spent some time in a psychiatric hospital in Barcelona. We were mostly out of touch during that period, but I saw him now and then after he returned to California. At one point he came to St. Louis for some kind of Cardinal function, and at the end of the evening he and I went out to a bar that we closed down at one or one-thirty in the morning. When they announced the last call, Curt went ballistic. I said, "Curt, they're closing." Didn't matter. He was outraged that he couldn't get another drink. Until that moment, I hadn't realized the full extent of his problem. He wasn't the same Curt Flood that I'd known so well over so many years.

It was later, when he was battling throat cancer—from smoking—that we really renewed our friendship. We'd e-mail, talk on the phone, meet at fantasy camps and the like. He once wrote me a poignant note about how he expected to beat the cancer. He died early in 1997, two days after his fifty-ninth birthday. Jesse Jackson gave the eulogy.

Curt's story was tragic, in the personal sense, but it was also essential on a level that makes him both historic and heroic. It set the narrative for a punishing process that had to occur in the interest of progress. Somebody had to take the brunt of it. Somebody, in effect, had to martyr himself, and Curt was the guy. He fully understood the ramifications of what he was doing.

The greater tragedy, to me, is that so many of the modern players who have benefited from Curt's sacrifice have no idea what he went through or even who he was. The fact is, while Curt lost his case and his career and the life in which he'd flourished, the players who came after him won and won big. In its sympathetic denial of Curt's specific lawsuit—the sticking point was that reserve clause could be overturned only by an act of Congress—the Supreme Court had stipulated that free agency in baseball should derive from collective bargaining. Salary arbitration, instituted in 1973, sprang from the negotiations that attended Curt's case. The 10/5 rule, by which a player with ten years of major-league service and five with his current team has the right to veto a trade, became known as the Curt Flood Rule.

Free agency, of course, arrived for real in 1976, when arbitrator Peter Seitz granted it to Andy Messersmith and Dave McNally after they had played a season without contracts. Much later, a year after Curt's death, Congress established the Curt Flood Act, which formally restricted Major League Baseball's antitrust exemption. A year after that, Curt was recognized by *Time* magazine as one of the ten most influential athletes of the twentieth century.

It would have been nice if he had still been around to soak up those acknowledgments—they'd have meant a lot—but precious moments had not been unknown to him. In 1992, he received the Jackie Robinson Award from the NAACP. And the most gratifying, perhaps, may have come in 1994, when he delivered a pep talk to the active players on the eve of their strike and they responded with a standing ovation. It was important for Curt to feel not forgotten; and it's important for me, too, to feel that he's not.

I should add that he jumped on Dobson's first pitch to him, a fastball middle-in, and with his short, efficient stroke, smacked it past Stanley into center field, a two-out single.

FOR ALL OF his wildness—which, frankly, had served him well, as it sometimes does in our line of work—Dobson had now thrown first-pitch strikes to three straight batters. Make it four. According to Gorman, his fastball to Maris caught the outside corner.

I'd have expected another fastball, because he'd been having trouble getting his curve over the plate until Brock abused one; because we'd already stolen two bases and beaten the throw on another; and, in that vein, because Flood had a sizable lead over at first. Naturally, Dobson dropped an off-speed curve to the bottom of Roger's knee, on the inside corner, called strike two.

Flood was plenty fast enough to score from first on a double, but Roger didn't hit many of those. He'd gone six straight years with fewer than 20. He'd also gone six straight years with fewer than 72 RBIs. It's somewhat remarkable that we'd won two straight pennants with him batting third in the order (although Flood had occupied that spot nearly as often in '68)—especially considering the subpar season our cleanup hitter had just struggled through. But we were a situational team, and Roger had become a situational player.

The situation in question changed on the next pitch, which came after Dobson checked on Flood and stepped off the rubber. When he returned to it, he opted for another curveball, also down and in, the kind that would make it difficult for Freehan to throw out Curt if he attempted to steal second. Which he did. Freehan's throw was high and inside, making Stanley leave his feet to catch it, by which point Flood had already left *his* to slide in untagged.

In this improved circumstance, Maris loomed larger than the sum of his recent numbers. We were all aware that the World Series would be his last hurrah, and it would surprise nobody— certainly not us or the St. Louis fans, to whom Roger had endeared himself by simply being himself—if he made it memorable. He was a rise-to-the-occasion kind of player, and had shown it the previous October against the Red Sox. Even with two strikes, I liked his chances here better than Dobson's.

He popped a fastball into the seats behind home plate.

In spite of the 4–0 lead, Flood's run, should he score it, would not be insignificant. I'd have to face the top of Detroit's formidable lineup once more, and at least some of its power. And I'd never been beaten or tied by a five-run homer.

Dobson handled the rosin bag, wiped his brow with both his sleeves, gave Flood a couple glances, and missed outside with a good running fastball.

The next pitch was a different thing altogether. I believe it was a breaking ball, but it was hard to tell because breaking balls don't bend much at high altitude. Freehan sprang in the air and was able to slow it down with the upper edge of his mitt, dissuading Flood from scooting to third.

At 3-and-2, the advantage may have been Dobson's. His necessity of delivering a strike was mitigated by the open base at first and the right-handedness of Cepeda, who would bat if Maris walked. With that leeway, he threw Roger a slider.

It wasn't a particularly good one, floating over the inner half at the numbers, but its merit was in the relative pace. Roger's swing was a tick ahead of the ball's arrival. He popped it softly to McAuliffe.

	1	2	3	4	5	6	7	8	9	R	H	E
Tigers	0	0	0	0	0	0	0			0	4	3
Cardinals	0	0	0	3	0	0	1			4	5	0

(Focus on Sport/Getty Images)

The '68 Series was the last time that Cepeda, our director of music and enthusiasm, would wear a Cardinal uniform. We would say good-bye to McCarver (being interviewed here by Tony Kubek of NBC) a year later, by virtue of the same trade that Flood refused to accept.

Eighth Inning

THERE WAS A time when Eddie Mathews hit me as hard as anyone in the National League. At thirty-six, slowed down years before by a shoulder injury and three months removed from mid-season surgery for a ruptured disk in his back, he was mostly a pinch hitter now—in this case, batting for Wert to lead off the eighth—but back in the day, Mathews had hit *a lot* of pitchers as hard as anyone in the league. And if he didn't, his running mate probably did.

Mathews and Aaron. Aaron and Mathews. For about a decade, starting in 1954—when Aaron was a rookie and Mathews was pictured on the cover of the first-ever *Sports Illustrated*—they followed one another, in either order, at the heart of the Milwaukee Braves' devastating lineup; third and fourth, back and forth, the home-run-hittingest teammates in baseball history. They left a pitcher no recourse. At least not *this* pitcher.

The deadliest duos around the league—Mathews and Aaron, Mays and McCovey, Clemente and Stargell, Williams and Banks—tended to be left-right combinations. Ordinarily, I'd tiptoe around the left-hander and make the right-hander beat me if he could. The complication with the Braves was that Aaron, the right-hander, happened to be the best fastball hitter in the universe. So I couldn't really fudge with Mathews. And it didn't go well for me, year after year.

Mathews was well established by the time I encountered him. He'd played the 1952 season in Boston before the Braves moved to Milwaukee, and he'd led the league in home runs, for the second time, when I was a rookie in '59. He would end up hitting only four homers against me altogether, but that didn't mean I got him out. As I did against most lefty sluggers, I steered clear of his wheelhouse, working him with fastballs on the outer half— this was before I'd found the courage and control to put a slider on the outside corner—to minimize the damage. But he'd just hook the ball between first and second base, time and again. Reach and pull, I called it. Mathews pulled everything, and pulled most of it hard. For a long while, he batted over .400 against me, and even after he tore the ligaments in his shoulder he wasn't slowing down much. Until one night I got lucky.

That night—I'll say it was between 1963 and '65, but don't hold me to it—I tried to bring a fastball off the plate inside, standard procedure to set up the fastball away, but left it on the inner half, at the belt. As it hurtled toward almost certain annihilation, I cringed; probably cursed to myself. Mathews took a ferocious rip. And missed. *Huh?*

I scratched my head and made a dicey decision. Having had no luck with him any other way, I was willing to chance that, strange as it seemed, I'd stumbled upon a hole in his swing— one that had remained hidden because what pitcher in his right mind is going to throw Eddie Mathews a belt-high fastball over the inner part of the plate? This was a guy whose swing had been described as perfect by no less than Ty Cobb. Nevertheless, I kept jamming him with four-seamers on the buckle, and he kept coming up empty. And the best thing about this fortuitous turn of events: not only had I broken the code for Mathews, but it meant that I could now go after him on a regular basis and give Aaron a wide berth. Win-win!

When Tony La Russa managed the Cardinals and brought me in for a little coaching and instruction during spring training, he purposely didn't ask me many questions in front of the players because he was never sure what I'd say. On one occasion, though, he did inquire if I'd ever intentionally walked anybody. I said, yeah, I walked Hank Aaron from time to time. La Russa was having an issue with some of his pitchers who resisted intentionally walking batters, and I gave him the answer he wanted. But I should have added that I intentionally walked Aaron only because he was very difficult to pitch around and only after I'd accidentally learned how to get Eddie Mathews out.

Mathews put in fifteen Hall of Fame years for the Braves, the last being their first in Atlanta. He was traded to Houston before the 1967 season, and then to Detroit the same August. The first time he walked into the Tigers' clubhouse—this was when they were brawling with the Twins, White Sox, and Red Sox for the American League pennant—he was halted by a message on the chalkboard that he found inappropriate, something to the effect that they'd win the thing in spite of Mayo Smith. Mathews erased it and followed up with a stern greeting to his new teammates, most of whom were impressed.

At that point of his career, Eddie was more of a presence than a threat. Before the '68 season began, it was determined that he'd play only a reserve role; but it was not an unimportant one. His biggest contribution might have come in Oakland, late May, when he outraced his teammates from the dugout to the mound and landed a knockdown punch to the face of Jack Aker. On consecutive days, the Tigers had seen Kaline's arm broken and Northrup hit in the head, and the ten-minute fight that Eddie started was dubbed by the home plate umpire, Ed Runge, as the best he had ever seen. Detroit won sixteen of its next twenty-one games, extending its lead over Baltimore from one game to six and a half.

Mathews was a noted tough guy—like so many of the Tigers, he'd received scholarship offers in football—and while Aker was far from the first player he'd leveled, the Oakland reliever was something of an exception in terms of profile. Eddie's specialty was mixing it up with other superstars, particularly rugged ones. Among his famous adversaries were Jackie Robinson, Frank Robinson—both of whom had exceeded the limits of how hard he would allow an opponent to slide into third base—and Don Drysdale, whom he battered in a scenario similar to the one with the A's.

The clobbering of Aker had shown, if nothing else, that Mathews still had some fight in him. His return in early September from his back surgery corroborated that. In his final season—like Maris, the World Series would be his swan song—Eddie seemed determined to go out swinging.

As far as I can recall, though, he didn't *come up* swinging in the eighth inning. The first two pitches were not preserved on the videotape, but they were a ball and a strike, and I have a pretty good notion of what and where. A little background on that: Mathews's penchant for pulling the ball traced all the way back to when he was a boy. The story goes that while his father shagged in the outfield, Eddie's athletic mother pitched batting practice, and he would be in serious trouble if he drove a ball up the middle. Given the fact that he had crossed the aisle as a close second only to Mel Ott in National League home runs by a left-handed hitter—and now trailed only Ruth and Ted Williams in that department overall—and the fact that his overwhelming preference, in hitting home runs, was to yank them out to right field, it seemed prudent not to feed his appetite in that regard. And so, even though I'd found a blind spot on his inside corner, I was mindful of not pushing my luck. By this time, Mathews had finally resigned himself to going the other way with strikes on the outer third, but that was still the safest part of the plate for a pitcher. I'm betting that I missed outside with the fastball, and then, determined to do better, tried again and got the call.

There was something to be said for pitching to a guy—this applied to no other hitter the Tigers would send to the plate in the Series—with whom I had some actual history. And there was *a lot* to be said for pitching to Eddie Mathews when he had reached the end of the line. I was wary, though, of a dramatic farewell. He was certainly capable of rising to an occasion. As formidable as the Braves had been during—and largely because of—Eddie's years in Milwaukee, he had played in the World Series only twice before, with a single home run to show for it; but it was one that bears noting. Game four, 1957. The Yankees had won two of the first three, had tied this one with two outs in the top of the ninth on a three-run homer by Elston Howard, and had taken the lead off Warren Spahn in the top of the tenth. In the bottom of the tenth, Milwaukee had retied the game on an RBI double by Johnny Logan, which brought up Mathews with one out. The Yankee reliever was a right-hander, Bob Grim. After Mathews came Aaron. What to do? Grim's dilemma was the same one that would bedevil me time after time. On this occasion, Aaron already had two hits in the game, including a three-run homer, and he'd been the National League MVP, so, even with first base open, Grim went ahead and took his shot with Mathews, who already had a couple RBIs on a double. The ball landed far beyond the right-field fence, and the Braves went on to win the Series in seven games.

With a four-run lead and another pinch hitter due up next, my options were not quite as grim, so to speak. I turned to the trusty fastball on the belt, and he lifted it foul to the right side and behind him, out of play.

I had one large advantage remaining. Having been gone from the National League for nearly two years, Mathews had not seen the shiny backdoor slider I'd become so proud of, the one McCarver was now calling for. Check this out, old buddy.

It was a good one, hard and smallish, dipping in from the outside corner. Eddie hesitated a moment before plunging into his emergency hack—the "oh, shit" swing. His hands were pulled in too close to his body, as if he'd been expecting something around the midsection, and his bat passed harmlessly over strike three.

IF YOU'RE COUNTING, which I wasn't, that made 14 strikeouts.

My reason for not knowing or caring had nothing to do with being humble, which I also wasn't, or politically correct, which I never even considered. I simply hadn't seen much of a connection between strikeouts and winning.

Only once in 1968 had I struck out 15 batters. It was maybe the worst game I pitched all year. It was definitely the most runs I gave up. And the biggest lead I blew.

I'm talking about the debacle I mentioned previously against the Pirates, when they beat me with three in the seventh inning (a three-run homer by Stargell *to left field*, which made it worse), one in the eighth, and two in the ninth (started by a double from Stargell) to end my twelve-week winning streak and make me impossible to get along with for a couple days. It didn't matter that three of the runs were unearned. It didn't matter that I struck out Clemente three times or fanned the side twice or at one point blew away Maury Wills, Matty Alou, Clemente, and Stargell in succession. Nothing mattered but the final score. For me, nothing ever did.

Over the years, quite a bit has been said and written about my competitiveness. I'm beholden to the teammates, opponents, and critics who have alluded to it and almost kept it relevant; but I'm even more beholden to the big brother who embedded it. The best thing I can say about my own competitiveness is that, giving myself the benefit of the doubt, it might have ranked second in our family to Josh's.

My father, Pack—that was also my first name until I grew up and changed it—was a hardworking carpenter and church man who died a few months before I was born. As a child, the seventh and last in the household, I suffered from rickets and pneumonia, and my mother, a laundress and housecleaner, pampered me as a result. I enjoyed the pampering. Josh, fifteen years older than I was, took it upon himself to balance things out.

He was the one who carried me in a quilt to the hospital and promised me a baseball glove if I beat the pneumonia; who built a pitcher's mound at our elementary school and showed me how to use it; who applied the Band-Aid and shoved me back onto the field after one of the fierce ground balls he drilled at me drew blood; who coached our neighborhood teams so willfully;

who refused, with all his heart, to be beaten, cheated, or demeaned, and expected the same of anyone who played for him—especially me.

His dedication to coaching was, of itself, a refusal to be beaten. When his World War II service in India was up, Josh earned a teaching degree at a college in the South, where he also ran track. But when he brought the degree back to Omaha, he couldn't land a teaching job. The neighborhood—basically the Logan Fontenelle housing project and rec center—became Josh's classroom. He went on to earn his master's at Creighton while coaching us, when I was fifteen, to the first state baseball championship that a predominantly black team had ever won in Nebraska. And don't think that we won it because I was on the mound. Most of the time, I wasn't. I threw fewer strikes than two other guys, so I caught, played shortstop and center field, pitched a little, and batted cleanup.

We won because Josh drove us to it. I mean, he worked and goaded and inspired us to win, but he also, literally, *drove* us. We played wherever we could get a game—Nebraska, Missouri, and a whole lot of Iowa. This was the late forties and early fifties, the towns were small, and as you can imagine, we weren't received with deference in most of them. That was okay, even with Josh, until it extended to the umpiring, at which point the tension had a way of escalating. My brother, a burly man with a deep, indelicate voice, held nothing back in his assessment of the ump's performance, and if the crowd turned against us, he would march out to the mound and invite the local folks to join him there. Getting out of town could be a challenge. Even on the occasions when our hosts attempted to be hospitable, there was no guarantee that it would end well. Once, after a game in Maryville, Missouri, we were invited to the town square for watermelon.

When Josh noticed some of the locals standing back and taking pictures of us gorging ourselves, he made us stop eating until forks were provided. Of course, none of us had ever eaten watermelon with a fork, but that was the rule from there on out: no fork, no watermelon. I loved watermelon as much as the next guy, but after I understood what was going on, I declined it altogether in those circumstances. I was a junior Josh, through and through.

Our whole family was pretty much that way, characterized by wide shoulders with chips on top. Even my sister Barbara Jean was someone you didn't want to mess with. When I was fairly young, there was a neighborhood bully named Donald who would chase me and my friend Rodney home from school every day, threatening to work us over if he caught us. I mentioned it to Barbara Jean, and she instructed us on what route to take the next day. When we reached a certain spot, she intercepted Donald and coldcocked him right in his tracks. He never bothered us again.

Five of the Gibson kids were boys, and when we came together as a basketball team, which wasn't often, we took no prisoners. Josh also played on an adult team he coached, and it was a lesson in aggression to watch him throw his bulk around. He was merciless. When his team was crushing the other one, he couldn't resist the spectacle of subbing in his little brother, the water boy. Even in a uniform several sizes too big for me, I wasn't timid about the opportunity, and was more than happy to pour it on.

I occasionally rebelled at the relentless way in which Josh pushed me, but I never lost sight of why he was doing it. When I was eleven, we'd talked about Jackie Robinson, and I had declared that I would become a professional athlete. Josh took me at my word and made sure I did everything in my power to achieve that goal. He certainly did everything in *his* power.

For that matter, I was not the only athlete he prepared for the pros in one sport or another. His rec center eventually became the YMCA, Josh was the program director, and the neighborhood stars he coached over the years included Gale Sayers (Pro Football Hall of Famer), Johnny Rodgers (Heisman Trophy winner), Bob Boozer (NBA all-star and Olympic gold medalist), and Marlin Briscoe (the first black man to start at quarterback in the American Football League). I was about a year and a half older than Boozer and really thought I'd be the first NBA player among us. After my senior season at Creighton, I filled out a questionnaire from the Minneapolis Lakers, but never heard from them again. All things being equal, I'd have chosen basketball over baseball—I loved it that much—and might even have stayed with the Globetrotters if they'd played some *real* basketball. They wanted me to be the dribbling specialist, like Marques Haynes and later Curly Neal, but I considered that to be clowning and wouldn't do it. I was wired to win.

Josh's youth basketball team, the Omaha Travelers, was every bit as good as his baseball teams. At one point the varsity squad from the University of Nebraska at Omaha came down to the YMCA to scrimmage us. We were all high schoolers with the exception of one older guy, and we beat the crap out of those college boys. When I stole the ball from their star and dunked it, he wanted to beat me up. With Josh on the sideline, that would have been a poor idea.

Needless to say, North Omaha was loaded. Our housing project alone could produce a track team that would win state. In a lot of low-income neighborhoods, status was measured in toughness. In ours, speed was the thing. At Logan Fontenelle, the large grassy plaza—ideal for football games and major fights—was encompassed by a sidewalk, which to us was a running track.

To me, personally, it was the hard stretch where I learned the indignity of losing; where I found out, basically, how much I hated it.

The next step was to learn what it took to win. That's where Josh came in, teaching by example, intimidation, and force of character. In competition, Josh was a bully. Even when he and I played basketball against each other, and he outweighed me by eighty or ninety pounds, he'd shove me, hold me, trample me, whatever it took for him to win. There was no circumstance in which he tolerated not winning. Later on, I was the same way—well, maybe a little less physical—with my daughters and son.

I can't say that I kept Josh's growling voice in my head when I faced Willie McCovey with two on, or the Detroit Tigers in the eighth inning of a World Series game, and I didn't search for his face in the crowd. Josh, in fact, wasn't at the '68 Series. We'd had a falling-out that seemed to worsen over the years. For a while, I'd leave him tickets to our games—which we had to pay for in those days—but avoid him afterward. Then he just stopped coming. It was rough.

But I never stopped listening to the instincts he had developed in me. And those instructed me, in no uncertain terms, what to do with a four-run lead and five outs to go.

Pour it on.

I CAN'T IMAGINE that another team, in another World Series, ever sent up back-to-back pinch hitters with the bona fides of Eddie Mathews and Gates Brown, now batting for Dobson.

I started him with a slider down and in, ball one.

Brown had scuffled in 1967, and as a result the Tigers decided that Mathews would be their principal left-handed pinch hitter in '68. Then, on day two of the season, after Mathews had already taken a turn, the man they called Gator was sent up in the ninth inning of a tie game with the Red Sox, the defending league champions, and clubbed a walk-off home run for Detroit's first of 103 victories. All year, he never stopped doing stuff like that.

He set an American League record with 18 pinch hits, half of them for extra bases. He batted .450 in that role and, notwithstanding the Year of the Pitcher, an absurd .370 altogether. In the first game of an August doubleheader, again against Boston, he was summoned with two outs in the bottom of the 14th inning and delivered another walk-off homer. He played the entire second game and ended it, too, this time with a ninth-inning single that drove in Stanley from third base and capped a four-run rally.

In spite of starting only sixteen games, Brown became the face of the Tigers' comeback magic. Naturally, there was clamoring for Smith to put the big guy in the lineup, but Brown had grown less familiar with his glove since his buddy Horton took over the left-field job in '65. He would play thirteen years, all with Detroit, and never see 500 at-bats in any one of them; only twice would he come to the plate more than 300 times. Gates completed his career as the AL's all-time leader in pinch hits and first overall in pinch home runs. Pressure was no problem, he told reporters, because "I'm square as an ice cube and I'm twice as cool."

At five-foot-eleven and 220 pounds, with thick round shoulders, massive forearms, and a bit of a belly—he was built a lot like my brother Josh—Brown had once been considered the fastest man on the Tigers' roster. He couldn't put that speed to much advantage on the bench, but he didn't complain. In fact, it seemed as though he'd come to enjoy his leisure time in the early innings. He made friends among the fans nearby, and was known to prevail upon them for a hot dog or two, maybe in exchange for an autographed baseball card. The clubhouse boys also fed his habit, and it all led to an often told urban legend with conflicting details. The prevailing version places the game in 1968 and has Gates working on a couple dogs at the end of the dugout, middle innings, when Smith unexpectedly called his name. He quickly stuffed the snack in his shirt, smoked a ball into the gap, slid headfirst into second base, and scrambled up with mustard stains on his uniform as the middle infielders doubled over in laughter. Other reports have the episode occurring at first base as Gates dove back to the bag on a pickoff attempt.

He was, in any event, a character, a favorite of fans and teammates, and a hitter with such conspicuous talent that the Tigers found him playing prison ball in Mansfield, Ohio, where he was serving time for breaking and entering. Until then, Brown's athletic feats were concentrated in high school football. When Horton asked him what he took in high school, Gates is said to have answered, "A little English, some math, some hubcaps, some wheel covers . . ."

The Tigers arranged to have him paroled ahead of schedule and placed Brown in the Northern League, which he proceeded to lead in triples, finishing behind only one other fellow in stolen bases, as well. He reached Detroit by age twenty-four and would last long enough to be the Tigers' first designated hitter in 1973. In 1978, he became their hitting coach.

Brown batted from a slightly open stance, planted toward the front of the box, and our scouting report classified him as a pronounced pull hitter. Flood was positioned more than fifty feet toward right field, the kind of exaggerated shift that I'd learned to ignore. When a pitcher tries to make a batter hit in the direction of an adjusted defense, he plays to the guy's strength. There's no need for that. If a hitter invariably pulls, it means—since most pitchers are not likely to be aiming for his sweet spot—that he's turning on the ball wherever it's thrown. With that in mind, I didn't concern myself with the alignment of the guys behind me. I just tried to make good, sensible pitches.

Another slider. This one didn't break as much horizontally as the first pitch to Brown, but ducked just under his knees, ball two.

I was committed now to throwing a strike. Brown bent forward, hands held low, as he waited; but not for long. Fastball at the knees, middle third of the plate. The best pinch hitter in the American League stepped toward first base, reached with his lumberjack arms, and defied our scouting report by poking at the ball with the end of the bat. Brock jogged in a few steps and caught it in short left-center.

It would be another four days, at the minimum, before I'd have to deal again with the imposing lefties on the Tigers' bench.

OUR ROMP TO the pennant seemed to be serving me well. Although I'd pitched more regular-season innings than ever before, they'd been on schedule and consequently hadn't depleted me with a late flurry.

It was a different lead-up from the one that preceded the '67 Series. I had plenty left for the Red Sox, but that was because I'd made only five starts—as in '68, none of them under the pressure of a pennant race—after breaking my leg in July. When we got to Boston, there was probably some rejuvenation at work.

My first World Series, in 1964, had been entirely different.

That one had suddenly flashed into view at the end of one of the craziest races on record, a desperate dash to the finish line between us, the Reds, the Giants, and the Phillies, who squandered a six-and-a-half-game lead over the final two weeks. The situation demanded that I pitch four innings out of the bullpen on the final day of the season, two days after I'd worked eight innings in a tough 1–0 loss to Alvin Jackson and the Mets. I started and finished game two of the World Series four days later, followed by game five (ten innings) on another three days of rest and game seven on two. Over a frantic period of twenty-two days, starting in late September, I packed in 56 of the most strenuous innings—other than the ones with Josh in my face—I would ever pitch. Youth, adrenaline, and occupational hunger worked hard on my behalf.

This time, though, there were no extenuating circumstances beyond the ferocious lineup on the other side. Having negotiated Mathews and Brown, I was still up against an example of that: the top of the order.

His last two times at bat, McAuliffe had rapped fastballs to the right side. One had been fielded, the other hadn't; but more important, there was a pattern, and it suggested that he had the fastball timed. As a result, his chances of seeing a slider—especially as the count moved along—were pretty good.

My curveball, on the other hand, had probably run its course for the day. I was grateful for its unexpected contribution, but would ask no more. Not in the sweaty eighth inning, with 111 pitches yapping at my elbow, tearing at my hands, and grinding on my toes.

None of that, however, was out of the ordinary. For competitive purposes, I felt fine. I felt *good*. The noise in my elbow was drowned out by the roars of the crowd. It was the *World Series,* the days of feeling no pain.

Besides that, I don't wish to imply for a minute that my elbow felt anything like the left one of the man whose strikeout record I was unknowingly chasing. Koufax's pitching motion came from straight over the top, with a muscular, wrenching pull on his curveball. He couldn't brush his teeth. I was a three-quarter thrower dependent more on torque and leg drive. The pain in my elbow was just a chronic annoyance that I assumed every pitcher dealt with. In periods when it was flaring up a little more than usual, I'd take some Butazolidin—which is not approved anymore, unless you're a horse—on days that I pitched, right after my warm-up. The rest of the time, I just plowed through it, which was the baseball way. Only occasionally, mostly early in my career, did my elbow actually hold me back in a ball game. There was a game against Cincinnati, for example, when it was acting up so much that I could hardly throw a fastball or hard slider; so I just tossed a bunch of slop up there. I thought I was doing all right, keeping it close, until I got a hit, moved along to second base, and exchanged pleasantries with the Reds' shortstop, Leo Cardenas, who had been my roommate during winter ball in Venezuela. "Bobby," Leo said, "you no throw shit. Why you out there pitching?"

In the long term, my forearm actually caused more aggravation than my elbow. That was from throwing the slider. It made my forearm as hard as a brick. I'd get cortisone shots for it now and then, but it wasn't an easy proposition. One time, the doc broke his needle trying to stick it in there.

The slider also did a number on my index finger. Every game, the fingernail would crack straight across, about halfway down, from the pressure I had to exert on the ball, and around July the nail would start to break apart. I'd put a Band-Aid on it between starts, and it would begin to heal, but the Band-Aid always had to come off for the next game. Healing, I guess, is why God invented the off-season.

Nearer the end of my career, my knees were a mess. I had surgery to repair cartilage in the right one, and afterward fluid would build up in there and I could hardly bend it. At one point, it had to be drained just prior to each of 17 starts in a row. The left one, by that time, was pretty much shot from all the landing and twisting I'd asked of it. But my knees were not yet a factor in 1968. And I suspect that the sum of the other inconveniences—including the big toe I always abused when I dragged it from the rubber—amounted to less trouble, on this particular day, than McLain's tender shoulder was giving him. It probably had something to do with his bases on balls.

My only walk, meanwhile, had come with two outs in the fifth, just before the bottom of the batting order. McAuliffe, by contrast, was followed by the heart of it. Unless I was suddenly overtaken by the conditions of the day, he would see strikes.

Eventually, that is. The first pitch, a fastball, ran quite a bit inside and low.

That called for the removal of my cap and a swipe across the forehead with my sleeve. And another fastball. Higher, this time—at the belt—and over the inner half. Swinging for all he was worth from that wacky open stance of his, McAuliffe fouled it straight back.

His big rip was still another reason to turn to the slider at this point. Working quickly, I put one just where I wanted it, inside corner on his thigh. He pounced and fouled it sharply to the right side.

Disregarding all the mixed signals from his stance, setup, and stride, McAuliffe seemed to be poised for the inside pitch. Intent now on sticking with the slider and advised to move it outside, I had two options. One was the backdoor slider that I'd become so attached to. The other was the Bob Purkey slider that I brought out only when stricken by an attack of reckless courage.

I was introduced to the Purkey slider at a pregame meeting in 1965, the only year Purkey pitched for the Cardinals. He was a veteran who had won a lot of games for the Reds by folding in a knuckleball with other odd stuff, including a slider that neither broke nor sank. We were playing the Braves that night, and when the discussion got around to Hank Aaron, Purkey told us that, strange as it sounded, he'd had a lot of luck against Hammering Hank with hanging sliders. When he heard that, Ken Boyer said, "Not with me playing third, you won't." But Purkey taught me how to throw a proper hanging slider. You *over*throw it. The spin makes it look like the pitch will break as sliders normally do, but the speed keeps it on a straighter course, which gives it the appearance of actually backing up. I could pull it off in the bullpen, and sometimes in a game I conjured up a Purkey slider accidentally, overthrowing. It usually worked. It especially worked during day games, when the hitters can see the spin better and expect the silly thing to act like a genuine slider. But it's a hard pitch to throw on purpose, and most of the time I didn't have the guts to try. The World Series was one of those times.

The backdoor slider to McAuliffe turned in from the outside corner and plunged quickly below his knees. He bent down to lift it to left field, where Brock drifted a few steps to his right for an easy catch of the twenty-fourth out.

———

DON MCMAHON, A big Irishman from Brooklyn and the Tigers' third pitcher of the afternoon, might have found the Indian summer to his liking. On chillier days, he was known to bundle himself so tightly in the bullpen that his teammates called him Nanook.

McMahon had been traded to his sixth team in late July. He was thirty-eight years old and would pitch until he was forty-four, retiring from the Giants with fewer relief appearances than only Hoyt Wilhelm, the great knuckleballer, and my old teammate Lindy McDaniel. Of the 874 games he graced over eighteen seasons, he started only two; but it certainly wasn't for a lack of getting people out. In '68, he'd put up a 1.98 earned run average, the very same as the year before. Three other years, he beat that number. These days, McMahon, who rang up 153 saves before there was any prestige or money attached to them, would most likely be considered a closer; if not, a premier, back-of-bullpen setup man. In our day, he was a workhorse journeyman. He was still throwing strikes at age fifty-seven, pitching batting practice for the Dodgers, when he suffered a heart attack and died a few hours later.

His first pitch to Cepeda nipped the inside corner and Orlando let it pass for strike one.

I wouldn't have minded the extra rest that a rally would afford, and I'd certainly welcome another run or two, but more than that I wanted to see our cleanup hitter and head cheerleader get going. Cepeda was our only legitimate match for the Tigers' power. There was some anticipation among us that he'd break out at Tiger Stadium, where the reachable right-field fence seemed tailor-made for his opposite-field swing, but I'd feel better about that prospect if I saw him tear into one, right now, like it was 1967. He'd had some previous success against Mc-Mahon, including a home run. Come on, Cha Cha.

McMahon missed outside with a high fastball, and then inside with a high, straight something-or-other, probably a sinking fastball. It looked like he wanted the call on that one, but a sinkerballer has no business arguing a pitch up there. I suspect that he might have been a little frustrated. McMahon's stuff was designed for the lower part of the zone and the Tigers seemed committed to pitching Cepeda high, which was actually the right thing to do, since he was a low-ball hitter. The last time around, though, Orlando had put a couple good rips on high fastballs from McLain and pulled them hard. It was promising.

The 2-1 pitch caught a little thigh and a lot of plate. Cepeda rocked, cocked, and knocked it into the sky, left side and close by. Dick Tracewski, having taken over at third base after Mathews pinch-hit for Wert, rushed forward into foul territory but stopped short as Freehan, tossing his mask aside, reached up with his catcher's mitt and made the play.

THE CARDINALS CALLED up McCarver when he was seventeen, a few months after he graduated from high school. In between, he went to Keokuk, Iowa, and tore up the Midwest League. This was 1959. It was my first year in the big leagues, too, although neither of us was there to stay. I was twenty-three.

Tim credits his sister with speeding his development, she being the one who coaxed him to bat left-handed. It helped, of course, that he caught, as well. In a little quirk of destiny, the first time he crouched behind the plate for Keokuk, the umpire breathing on his neck was Brent Musburger. Tim must have picked up some broadcasting tips and remembered them well, because my old friend has announced more World Series games on television than Curt Gowdy or anyone else, has won six Emmy Awards, and made it to the Hall of Fame by sharing the kind of insight that I used to shoo him off the mound for. And all that occurred after he became the first catcher of the twentieth century to play in four decades—a distinction he wouldn't have attained had he not joined us just before the fifties let out.

His 1,909-game career began in Milwaukee as a two-out, ninth-inning pinch hitter on September 10. The Braves' pitcher was the 215-pound right-hander he would face in the eighth inning of October 2, 1968. McMahon threw even harder back then, and he was about to lead the National League in saves. Tim fell behind 2-and-0. McMahon then threw a curveball—I can't imagine why—and McCarver looped it to right field, where it was caught, to end the game, by Hank Aaron, one of his heroes. When Aaron had come to bat in the first inning, Tim had stood up in the dugout and urged him on with an enthusiasm that was not endorsed by the other Cardinals. He was an excitable kid.

Three days later, batting leadoff against Glen Hobbie of the Cubs, McCarver beat out a grounder for his first major-league hit. He would not win a regular place in our lineup, however, until 1963, after the club had traded Gene Oliver—the only Cardinal who could hit Koufax—to make room for him.

While we were sorry to lose Oliver's special talent, we were happy with our new catcher, and very happy in October of '64 when Tim batted .478 against the Yankees and won game five for us, and me, with his three-run, tenth-inning home run against Pete Mikkelsen. We also enjoyed his imitation of the Crazy Guggenheim character from *The Jackie Gleason Show*.

Now, with one out in the eighth, the first pitch he saw from

McMahon zipped low and inside. McMahon had a smooth, easy delivery, and he was throwing a high percentage of fastballs, sinking or otherwise. The second was also off the inside corner but considerably higher, not far from Tim's ribs, and he popped it back behind the screen.

Awaiting the 1-1, McCarver squeezed the bat, stepped out of the box, and walked over to the batboy for some pine tar to rub on his hands. Ready again, he let two more fastballs go by, one inside—in the very spot of the pitch that Tim had fouled—and the other high.

Even at 3-and-1, it was unlikely that Tim would walk. He had done that only 26 times during the season; and most years, he struck out even less frequently. He was a good contact hitter, especially for a catcher—although not as good as the guy who succeeded him in 1970. Joe Torre manned the position most of that season, and hit at an All-Star level. (Joe would move to third base the next year, when he led the National League with a .363 batting average.) I was all for teammates who could hit—I *loved* teammates who could hit—and Joe Torre remains one of my favorite people in the world, but I had developed a special rapport with Tim, and that's the kind of thing that simply can't be replaced.

What's more, I wasn't the only one who felt that way about him. As much as the trade of Flood ultimately shook up the game of baseball, the trade of McCarver, in the same deal, shook up the Cardinals. Tim was a guy who held us together, and when he was suddenly gone, we missed him badly. Of course, being ballplayers, we had a peculiar way of showing it. Playing for the Phillies in 1971, Tim dropped a foul pop near our dugout and some razzing ensued. That, in turn, was followed by a couple brushback pitches to Brock. Lou said something about it to Tim, Tim answered in a physical way, and when the dust settled, McCarver was ejected.

He returned to the Cardinals for the 1973 season and most of '74, my last two years as a full-time starter, but was back with the Phillies in 1975, when he carved out a niche that extended his career: He caught Steve Carlton. Now and then he might strap on the gear for Randy Lerch or Larry Christenson, but his basic job description was Carlton's personal catcher. Lefty, as Steve was known, had tailed off a little since his incredible 1972 season, in which he went 27–10 for a team that won only 59 games, but all was well when he paired up again with Tim. In 1977, Carlton won his second Cy Young Award and McCarver batted over .300 for the first time since the minor leagues.

In 1980, when Carlton set about on his third Cy Young season—he had one more still to come—McCarver was describing it from the Phillies' broadcast booth. Late in the season, though, he squeezed into a uniform to add the eighties to the three decades he'd already played in. He even mixed in a hit, a two-run double in the last game of the season.

By 1985, Tim was back in the World Series, taking over after ABC fired Howard Cosell. His last Series, for Fox Sports in 2013, was a reprise of 1967—Cardinals and Red Sox—with a different result. The next year, at age seventy-two, he came home to call a limited number of the Cardinals' local telecasts.

It was a long journey from that first fly ball against Don McMahon, who now put a fastball on the inside corner at McCarver's belt. Tim slapped it in the direction of Cash, who fielded the ball to his right on the second bounce. Breaking from the mound on contact, McMahon took Cash's overhand throw in perfect stride and crossed first base one step ahead of Crazy Guggenheim.

AS I WRITE this, it occurs to me that, between them, McCarver and Shannon—the Christian Brothers—have been broadcasting baseball games for seventy-eight seasons. As a team, we never lacked for something to say.

Shannon's second career was moved up by a kidney condition that sadly brought his playing days to an end in 1970. By 1971, the only remaining members of our starting eight from '68 were Brock and Maxvill (Javier still played some second base, but Ted Sizemore played more). Aside from me, the only holdover from the '68 pitching rotation was Carlton (who won 20 games for the first time). Before the 1972 season, Carlton was dealt to the Phillies and Javier to the Reds. By the time it was over, Maxvill had been traded to Oakland. By the spring of '73, it was just Lou and me. The order of departure, including top reserves and relievers, had been Maris; Johnny Edwards; Tolan and Wayne Granger together; Larry Jaster; Dick Schofield; Ed Spiezio and Ron Davis together; Cepeda; Dick Hughes (all of those before the 1969 season began); Mel Nelson; Ron Willis; Flood, McCarver, and Hoerner together; Dave Ricketts; Ray Washburn (prior to 1970); Phil Gagliano; Shannon; Briles (prior to 1971); Carlton; Javier; and Maxvill.

That's a big part of the reason why I savor the 1968 team. We considered ourselves a unique group of guys—I don't think I'm being presumptuous to say straight-out that we *were*—and, although we couldn't know it at the time, the '68 World Series was our last shot together. His career having ended in the unforeseen manner that it did, I'm sure that Shannon, a lifelong Cardinal lover besides, feels the same way I do about that club, and that time.

He yanked a fastball foul, and when McMahon followed with

a humpback curve away from him, at the knees, Mike poked it past Stanley and into center field for his second hit of the day, a clean two-out single.

WHEN THE NINTH inning arrived, the fourth batter for the Tigers would be Willie Horton. It meant that if the two, three, and four hitters in the Detroit lineup—Stanley, Kaline, and Cash—happened to reach base, the tying run would be represented by a guy who had just hit more homers than anybody in the National League.

This made me an ardent supporter of Julian Javier, who was batting .370 in his World Series career. Hoolie had already driven in a couple runs back in the fourth, and I was solidly in favor of another, right here. A double down the line would do the trick. Either line. If I could somehow convince him that McMahon was left-handed . . .

He reached down to pick up some dirt, rubbed it in his hands, adjusted his helmet, stepped into the batter's box, smoothed a place for his feet, stepped out, spit on his hands, rubbed them together again, readjusted his helmet, and stepped back in, all for reasons that only Javier knew for sure. This was a guy who once slid safely into second base, stood up, listened to something the shortstop, Julio Gotay—a former teammate of ours—whispered in his ear, then jumped off the bag and was tagged out. When he got back to the dugout, we of course asked him what the hell happened. He just waved his arms around saying, "Voodoo! Voodoo!" He refused to go back out to the infield—"No! No! No!"—until we somehow calmed him down.

Hoolie took a two-seamer away, stepped out, did his thing, and swung at the following fastball, this one centered, fouling it straight back. That surely must have at least tied the World Series record for fouls straight back by both teams.

At 1-and-1 my favorite second baseman put his bat behind his back and stretched for a moment before spitting into his hands and adjusting his helmet. It was a fastball again, higher than the last, and Hoolie sent it into the air to the right of Northrup, who started fast, slowed down, called off Horton, and squeezed the out that summoned me to the mound for the ninth time.

Pedal to the metal.

	1	2	3	4	5	6	7	8	9	R	H	E
Tigers	0	0	0	0	0	0	0	0		0	4	3
Cardinals	0	0	0	3	0	0	1	0		4	6	0

(AP Photo)

By the ninth inning, having been struck out fourteen times, the Tigers were swinging more aggressively than they had earlier. This was my 138th pitch, a 2-2 slider on the inner edge of the plate, and Norm Cash, Detroit's cleanup hitter, took a hefty whack at it.

Ninth Inning

IT WAS MY twenty-seventh ninth inning of the year, my 116th pitch of the day, and my first curveball in a while. Or at least my slowest slider in a while. A slurve, you might call it. By whatever name, a breaking ball. On the hands. Stanley took a late, abbreviated swing and tapped a roller along the first-base line, where Cepeda picked it up in foul territory.

Last time up, he'd also checked his swing on a breaking ball, a slider that was called for a strike on the outside corner. I now had in mind another one of those. This time, though, it was *off* the outside corner and a little low.

Let's try that again.

Farther outside and lower besides.

This was why I threw fewer breaking balls in the late innings. The action was there, but not the command. I was well into my third hour of driving off my right leg, pivoting hard on my left, whipcording my arm, and sweating down my chin. I was tuckered. When you're worn out and the springs in your legs have lost some oomph, there's a tendency to compensate by pushing too hard and overdoing it. Overstriding. A longer stride means a better chance of hanging a breaking ball. And so, when the ninth innings came around, I typically loaded up on fastballs. People used to remark that I threw harder in the ninth inning than I did in the first. Not true. I just erred on the side of the fastball.

That's what Stanley would see next, at 2-and-1. In this scenario, I wasn't particularly concerned about hanging a breaking ball that he'd smack out of the park, even though he was capable of that—with a four-run lead, a solo home run would not be devastating—but I was determined not to walk him. Not leading off the ninth ahead of Kaline, Cash, and Horton. All year long, I'd walked only two batters in the ninth inning. One of those was intentional.

The ninth, in fact, had been one of my better innings all-around. For the season, my ninth-inning ERA was 0.69. The only ninth-inning home run against me came from a part-time outfielder with the Cubs named Al Spangler, who played for thirteen years and never hit more than five homers in any of them. The one off me in August, which accounted for half his season's total, tied the game. I ended up pitching 11 innings and we lost in 13. The memory makes me sick to my stomach. I can understand how the home run happened, though, because Spangler was leading off the inning—just like Stanley now—and he was the kind of guy I wouldn't be extra-careful with, the kind whom I'd be deadly serious about not walking. The other side of the coin is that I hadn't given up a ninth-inning home run all year to an actual home run hitter. In light of the several who would follow Stanley, that was reassuring.

My pattern against Stanley had been to start him inside, then work him away. Having started him inside this time, I had no more immediate plans for that part of the plate. But I needed to locate the *other* part.

I took McCarver's throw and turned my back to him, muttering to myself. The ninth was my inning for muttering. As a rule, I said next to nothing for seven innings; maybe had a word or two of self-encouragement or condemnation, either one, in the eighth; and carried on a quiet, single-person pep talk in the ninth. It was my way of coaxing myself through the fatigue. "Okay now, let's go. Come on, Hoot."

Turning back to Tim, I wiped my face with my sleeve, waited for Stanley, and placed a fastball on the outer half. He fouled it back.

In the pattern of the afternoon, there were likely to be more fastballs, and more fouls back. Stanley stepped away and picked up some dirt, watching me as he rubbed it in his hands. He banged his spikes with his bat, returned to the box, reached for another fastball on the outer half, and fouled it back.

The crowd groaned on contact. I felt the same way, although, as I would later understand, for different reasons.

The next fastball was a little higher, more centrally located. Stanley swung heartily and once again—enough of that!—fouled it back. This wasn't helping.

To me, what made the ninth inning so hard, start after start, was that it followed the *hardest* inning. And what made the eighth the hardest inning was that it preceded the ninth. I always knew that if I could make it to the ninth, I'd be in position to finish the game, so I poured everything into the twenty-second, twenty-third, and twenty-fourth outs. I knew also that the effort would leave me with less to work with in the ninth, which would become an exercise in endurance, adjustment, resourcefulness, and will. And fastballs.

More dirt for Stanley, followed by another fastball from me, in the same vicinity as the previous one but a smidgen higher. The swing was different, but the outcome was not. Foul back.

Stanley was staying alive against some pitches I couldn't complain about. It was a good at-bat on his part, and a hell of a time for it. He seemed to have the fastball timed. If this were the first or fourth or even the seventh inning, a slider would have been the ticket here.

Same fastball. Same damn foul.

He had not officially won the battle, but Stanley would be seeing his ninth pitch, and for him there was some triumph in that, a toll exacted from a tired opponent. For my part, I'd concede him the wear and tear and be more than happy with the twenty-fifth out. Okay, Hoot. Come on, let's go.

Having put my body through the wringer, Stanley now went to work on my head. Stepped out. Made me wait. Studied me. Decided on a fastball.

On that, we agreed. It was a two-seamer, but too high, too centered, to serve its purpose. Stanley slapped it on one bounce to Flood, a clean leadoff single.

AS INTENDED, MAYO Smith's lineup gambit was causing me aggravation. Between them, Stanley and Kaline had three of the Tigers' five hits, including the only one for extra bases. And now, with 124 pitches having been poured from my tank and still no outs in the ninth inning, the ad hoc shortstop took his lead at first base, making me operate from the stretch position as the greatest Tiger of the generation, eager to make a mark on his first World Series, dug in with the confidence of a Hall of Fame hitter whose last swing had produced a hard double down the left-field line.

I much preferred the full windup. In addition to any distraction or discomfort it might have caused the hitter, it gave me rhythm, momentum, and drive. My careening motion was more than a signature; it was a vehicle. A method. *My* method. To me, the windup was like getting a running start—Happy Gilmore on the tee. In the ninth inning especially, when I depended on fastballs and needed all the lower-body assistance I could get, I wanted to step back, whirl forward, and fling myself as fully as possible into every last pitch.

That said, I wasn't so bad with a runner on base. In '68, the batting average against me had been .191 with at least one man on, as opposed to .180 without. My control was slightly better from the stretch, which figures. That's the reason modern pitchers have streamlined their motions, after all.

I picked up the rosin bag, wiped my face, adjusted my cap, gave Stanley an obligatory look at first base—he was going nowhere and Cepeda wasn't holding him on—and held the ball for a beat or two between my belt and chest. Having gotten behind Stanley on breaking stuff and suffered the consequences, I went straight to the fastball for Kaline. It was on the inner half and he whaled at it, cooling the park and coming up empty.

Now I could throw a slider. The one he'd slammed for a double in the sixth inning had dipped sharply but stayed over the plate. This slider was flatter, on the outer half above the knees, with plenty of steam but less break than I anticipated. Kaline swung hard again, again missing.

My favorite count. A murmur from the crowd. Me oblivious to it, aware only of McCarver's sign. Harry Caray proposed to the viewing audience that I would now come with the mustard. It would have been more impressive if he'd said that I would now come with the mustard just off the outside corner, hoping for a swing at a pitch that couldn't be hit very hard.

I pulled it too far off the corner. Ball one. Groans all around.

There was one more ball available before the slider would be out of the equation. I deferred, instead, to the inning, weather, and pitch count, throwing a two-seamer that would have been ball two, low and maybe outside, if Kaline hadn't been protecting the zone and then some. The beauty of two strikes and fewer balls. He reached and fouled it off to the right side.

I sensed now that I didn't *need* to throw the slider. With Kaline up there swinging, a fastball just out of his hitting range would accomplish the same thing as a comparably placed slider that I was more likely to make a mistake with. I drew in some air, filled my cheeks, blew it out, and cast my lot with a fastball at the letters. Kaline cut loose and fouled it back.

McCarver, who probably noticed me catching my breath, removed his mask and advanced a few steps in my direction, shouting encouragement or wisdom or time-consuming nonsense, I'm not sure which. My response, when he returned to his post, was to shake him off—after three straight fouls, I reserved the right to change my mind about the fastball—and turn, at last, to the slider.

It was pretty much the same pitch that had ended badly for me in the sixth. Maybe it broke slightly more and sank slightly less; but mostly it was just a *slider*. That's what made Kaline miss, with a lovely rip, for his third strikeout of the afternoon.

As I wiped my forehead, the men in their white shirts and skinny ties, and the ladies, too, stood up to holler and applaud, as if the inning were now over, the game suddenly won. *What's the matter with these people?* And I'll be damned if there wasn't

McCarver again, walking my way. *What the hell? I'm getting on a roll here. Come on, let's go!*

Tim was pointing out to left-center field. What, did Flood run to the bathroom or something? Did Morganna, the Kissing Bandit, bounce out there to lay one on Brock?

The *scoreboard*. Fifteen strikeouts, it said. I'd tied the World Series record by Koufax. Well, hooray.

I COULD SEE that this wasn't going to stop until I took my stretch and got started on Cash. I probably hurried the pitch, my rhythm busted. It was a four-seamer, too high, ball one.

The next one was higher than the first, but Cash whiffed at it.

Notwithstanding Stanley's single, and in spite of all the thunder in the middle of the Tigers' order—actually, *because* of it— the ninth inning was now setting up nicely. The big boppers tend to swing harder and more often than singles hitters. These guys were hacking. Better yet, they were chasing. After being shut down for eight innings, they had come out aggressively for the last time around, intent on hitting a ball early in the count so they didn't fall behind. Fortunately for me, they hadn't taken into account that, by the ninth inning, my command would be straying a bit. They were enabling me to ring up strikes without actually throwing them.

A slider now, looking like a fastball—which is what makes it work—on Cash's hands, the perfect spot. No straying this time. Tim had set his target in the middle of the zone and I'd aimed at it, trusting the ball to break, as it did, across the inside corner. To my immense satisfaction, it was a fifth-inning pitch four innings later. And a swing and miss, strike two, with background music, the rumble of a capacity crowd.

I'd unlocked a secret. To beat ninth-inning burnout, all you have to do is tie a strikeout record: The energy will wash over you from all around the ballpark. When I pulled abreast of Koufax, the effect was game-changing. After eight-plus innings of wretched humidity, the atmosphere was now dispensing nourishment. For a moment, my exhaustion had fled the scene. Let's play two!

I put a fastball in the same spot as the slider, and Cash popped it foul about eight rows behind our dugout, with Tim giving chase as though he had a chance to catch it, bless his heart.

By the time he got into the squat again, I was ready. The urging Cardinal fans played the role of the nice people along the route of a marathon, cheering on the runners and handing out orange slices, but there was always a little extra spring in my step when I caught sight of the finish line. It was time to get this done, and the sooner the better.

With his mitt and open hand, Tim motioned for me to slow down. I counted to three and gave Cash a backdoor slider that caught more of the outer half than I'd intended. He slashed it foul the other way.

Another inside slider, lower than before. In the main, I considered a knee-high slider on the inside corner to be a bad idea when pitching to a strong left-handed hitter like Cash, who could drop his barrel on it and whistle it over Cepeda's head, or maybe Maris's. Fortunately, this one carried several inches off the plate. Cash, well in front, yanked it foul.

As pumped as I was, my body knew damn well that it had thrown 136 pitches in steamy conditions. The last two had missed their marks to the point of concern.

I twitched off the slider call and Tim set up for a fastball on the outside corner. It wasn't close. Wrong side of the plate, at shoe level. Cash nearly swung.

After a pitch like that, my catcher didn't have to tell me to slow down. I turned around, bent over, picked up some dirt, removed my glove, tucked it under my elbow, rubbed the ball, grabbed a breath, turned back around, and took my stretch knowing two things: Cash was anxious and I was due.

With a grunt and a stiff wrist, I let it fly. *There! That's* the slider I'm looking for! Inside corner again, imitating a fastball, but higher than the last one—headed toward Cash's wheelhouse, matter of fact. The meat of his bat was directly on it, a microsecond ahead, and then, *poof,* the ball was gone; not over the right-field fence, where his big swing would have sent it if the pitch hadn't acted as it did, but straight down, into the sweet spot of my buddy's beautiful mitt.

The St. Louisans were on their feet again, yelling deliriously, and this time I could have joined them, as great as it felt. My pleasure, though, didn't come from the new strikeout record, which was the reason folks were carrying on as they were, thank you very much; it came from the *pitch.* The 16th K was very nice and all that, but the leap in my heart was a product of the ninth-inning, second-out, disappearing *slider.* Yeah!

By now, of course, I knew what the big fuss was about, and wasn't quite so annoyed. I even took my cap off, although I disguised the gesture by wiping my forehead. Not wishing to encourage the interruption but welcoming the refreshment it provided, I let it play out. But I did so from the rubber, awaiting Willie Horton.

———

THE REAL SIGNIFICANCE of those two strikeouts was that, had Kaline and Cash put the bat on the ball and done so safely, the muscleman at the plate would have a chance to wipe out our lead.

Horton seemed to be getting better swings as the game wore on. In the seventh, he'd smashed a fastball to Maxvill. On the other hand, he hadn't been particularly discriminating, and the way the Tigers were up there ripping in the ninth, I had no reason to facilitate his power.

I left a four-seamer outside, and he laid off it.

As Horton chomped on his gum and set himself for the second pitch, a loud boom sounded somewhere in left field, followed by smoke that drifted over Flood's head in left-center. Malfunctioning fireworks that were supposed to have gone off after Brock's home run an inning and a half ago? Didn't know and didn't care. Until I watched the video, I never saw the smoke, and I can't say for certain that I even heard the salvo, as Harry called it—it took a lot more than a big noise to get my attention when the right pitch could end the game right *now*—but I did pause for a moment as the situation reset, keeping my eyes on Tim's sign and target.

We chose to improve upon the previous fastball, and did. Horton reached for this one, on the outer half of the plate, and added to the vast collection of foul balls that had accumulated in the box seats.

He was taking his time now, as he liked to do. Less proficient at fidgeting, I wiped my hand on my pants, checked to see that Flood was still there, tugged at my socks, and took my deepest breath of the day. If audience participation and twenty-six outs made me forget my fatigue, stalling batters reminded me. Lordy. I was highly motivated to make this the last guy; better yet, the last *pitch*.

I nominated a fastball and threw it high or outside or both. Horton, reminding me of what Kaline and Cash had done this inning and what Dizzy Dean had said before the Series about Willie's free swinging, went for it anyway, and of course fouled it back.

Now, a single pitch could do it in multiple ways. McCarver strolled out a few steps and held up one finger. Gorman brushed the plate. Horton stood outside the batter's box taking half swings, tightening his glove, adjusting his helmet.

As I stretched and pretended to look in Stanley's direction at first base, Tim set up just off the outside corner for the slider, which meant that I'd start it on the corner and hope that Horton would swing as it broke off the plate. I did my part; a damn good pitch, under the circumstances. Horton neglected to do his, although it crossed his mind for a moment. Two-and-two.

McCarver must have liked that slider as much as I did. While I grabbed one more deep breath, he called for the same pitch and set up in the same spot.

This time, I fell victim to the ninth-inning nemesis. I over-compensated. Overthrew. Left the pitch clear on the other side of the plate. I treated Willie Horton to one of those way-off, haywire breaking balls that meet no familiar criteria, follow no established order, and arrive with no prescription for how to handle. Willie elected to keep his bat held high behind his ear, assuming fastball and flinching noticeably as the wandering slider swerved from his lower left thigh to the edge of the inside corner.

Gorman's arm shot dramatically upward, and Tim was shaking my hand around the time it came down. By then, proceeding on from my follow-through, I was approaching the first-base line at a steady clip.

	1	2	3	4	5	6	7	8	9	R	H	E
Tigers	0	0	0	0	0	0	0	0	0	0	5	3
Cardinals	0	0	0	3	0	0	1	0	x	4	6	0

(AP Photo)

Roger Maris had warned us that Mickey Lolich, not McLain, was the
Tiger pitcher we had to worry most about. He was right.

Postgame

IN THE FIRST inning of the fifth game, which Brock had started with a double that enabled Flood to single him in, Cepeda gave us all we could ask for. As we'd hoped, the sight of Tiger Stadium had brought Cha Cha to life. He'd homered in Game 3, and now, rocking into a one-out pitch from Mickey Lolich, Detroit's lumpy left-hander, he hammered the ball well beyond the wall in left-center field, giving us an early 3–0 lead on the day when the world championship was ours to carry home for the second year in a row.

But we'll come back to that.

Lolich was the pitcher whom Roger Maris, a wise man, had warned us about. He'd beaten us in Game 2—when the temperature, by the way, had dropped into the *fifties*—and in the process rattled Nelson Briles with the only home run he would ever hit in his sixteen-year career. Cash and Horton also went deep that day, and Lolich, who'd been 10–2 over the last couple months of the season and was eager to get out from under McLain's shadow, allowed us only six hits in an 8–1 shellacking.

Nevertheless, the Series had remained in our grasp. We'd

quickly set things right in Tigertown, as Detroit was referred to on billboards all over the city. Kaline's two-run homer had put the Tigers ahead in Game 3, but McCarver trumped him with a three-run shot in the fifth. Cepeda matched that in the seventh, Brock did his thing with three hits and three steals, and Joe Hoerner, entering the game with a 4–3 lead and two runners on base, finished it with nearly four terrific innings of scoreless, one-hit relief.

Game 4 had been my province; and McLain's, as well. His shoulder was hurting, but unless he drank a carton of Pepsi before he went to bed, I assume he slept better than I did. At two in the morning, somebody knocked on the door of my hotel room yelling about a telegram. At three, somebody called asking for McLain.

But at least it gave me something to be angry about. This time around, McLain hadn't supplied any provocative remarks like he did before the Series began, when he spouted off about demolishing us. His tone had changed immediately after the opener, which, he said, he didn't feel badly about losing because I had pitched so well. The rest of the Tigers had been just as kind (unlike the Red Sox the year before in the same situation, when Yastrzemski muttered that a six-year-old could have gotten him out and he couldn't wait to meet up with me again). Cash called me Superman. Kaline and Horton—McCarver says he can still hear Willie gasping when that last slider of Game 1 snapped over the inside corner—told reporters that they'd never seen anybody pitch like that. Northrup added that there wasn't a man alive who could have hit me that particular afternoon.

It was all very generous of them, but I'd have preferred to play a team of jackasses. I'd have preferred a good night's sleep. I'd have preferred to not sit around for more than half an hour in a rain delay before the game could start. Then again, what the hell—it was the World Series. If you can't get yourself worked up for the World Series, you have no business pitching in it. I was ready enough; and when Brock led off the game with a long home run, I was downright rarin' to go.

In the third, McCarver tripled, Shannon doubled, and it was 4–0 when the umpires and commissioner cleared the field for another rain delay, which lasted nearly an hour and a quarter. While I was working a crossword puzzle, putting away a couple ice cream bars, and listening to Cepeda's jazz albums—the ones my accomplices and I hadn't stolen, because he had stacks of them given to him by a friend who worked for a record company and we knew he'd never miss a few here and there—McLain was informing Mayo Smith that his shoulder was done for the day. He later told reporters that he probably wouldn't pitch again in the Series, and we were on our way to making sure of it. I wanted full participation in that effort, and although it was common for a starting pitcher to pack it in after so long a stoppage, Schoendienst and I never entertained the notion.

When the game resumed, Joe Sparma was on the mound for Detroit. I homered against him leading off the fourth, making me the first pitcher to hit two in World Series play, I'll have you know. Of course, with the continuing threat that the rain could wipe everything out before the game made it to five innings and became official, I might have been wiser to take three wild swings. Later in the inning, after we'd scored another run, Cepeda walked and got himself sacrificially thrown out stealing second.

Trying to hurry along the bottom of the inning, I was careless to Northrup, who penalized me with a home run to make it 6–1. In the fifth, Javier singled with two outs and then came up with his own variation of the Cepeda maneuver, getting himself picked off—he lit out for second with the pitcher, Daryl Patterson, still holding the ball—to bring the Tigers to bat as quickly as possible. When they went down one-two-three, we were in the clear.

The rain kept coming, but with the game official, it felt a whole lot better than the mugginess of Game 1; and better still when we extended the lead. I came through with a ringing RBI on a bases-loaded walk in the eighth and then flashed my awesome North Omaha speed while scoring on Brock's double to make it 10–1, the final score. Brock had another three hits, everything but a single—he was truly amazing—and McCarver kept rolling with three of his own.

For all the delays and lopsidedness, Game 4 became the highest-rated sports program in television history to that point. And on the subject of records, I'll note, for the record, that I ended the day with a couple more myself, in addition to the home run thing. One was my seventh straight World Series win, which put me ahead of Red Ruffing and Lefty Gomez, both Yankees, and also broke the National League record for total World Series wins that I'd set in Game 1, when I passed Christy Mathewson and Three Finger Brown. By sticking through the entire four hours and twenty-five minutes from the original starting time, I established a new National League mark for consecutive complete games in World Series play. And my 10 strikeouts—three of them were Freehan, which was very nice considering what a tough out he'd been for me four days earlier—added to the league record for career World Series strikeouts that I'd broken back in the second inning of October 2, slipping past Koufax. I might have known it at the time if they'd put it up on the scoreboard.

———

THE MAIN THING, though, was that Game 4 put us up three games to one, and we were hopeful that José Feliciano's improvisational and highly controversial national anthem before Game 5—it might blend right in nowadays, but I'd never heard anything like it, and neither had anybody else—would be the last one we'd stand at attention to in 1968. Briles was pitching for us, and although he'd struggled a bit in Game 2, we knew that Nellie could get this done (he had come through with a complete-game victory against the Red Sox in the '67 Series and followed it up by winning 19 games in his first full season as a starter, impressing everybody with his command, his singing voice, and his imitation of Richard Nixon). Then Cepeda put us up 3–0 in the top of the first.

Yes, I'm back to that.

Stanley and Horton tripled in the fourth, and with two outs the Tigers scored their second run when a ground ball by Northrup took a bad hop over Javier's head. But it appeared that we were going to answer in the fifth when Brock—who in Game 4 had tied his own World Series record with his seventh stolen base— banged his second double of the day and Javier then dropped a single into left field. Horton charged the ball, fielded it on the first bounce, and, remembering what Stanley had told him about Brock neglecting to slide on plays like that, uncorked a strong one-hop throw to Freehan. Stanley was right. Brock attempted to score standing up, arriving at the plate at the same instant as Horton's throw. Freehan caught the ball and tagged Lou's hip in the same motion, their shoulders colliding as it happened. Doug Harvey, the supremely confident Hall of Fame umpire, raised his right arm and punched downward, signaling that Lou was out. Flood, who was on deck, was the first to jump in and argue.

Joe Schultz, our third-base coach, was next, followed by Brock and Schoendienst. To this day, Lou insists that he was safe, and I can't say that he was wrong. But I do wish he would have slid.

It was still 3–2 in the bottom of the seventh when Lolich, of all people—he was a career .110 hitter—stroked a single into right field and Briles was replaced by Joe Hoerner, who had pitched so sensationally in Game 3. Not this time. In rapid succession, McAuliffe singled, Stanley walked, Kaline singled, and Cash singled, giving Detroit a 5–3 lead.

There was no scoring in the eighth inning, and McCarver started the ninth with a leadoff single. Ed Spiezio, batting for Maxvill, delivered a one-out hit in his only plate appearance of the Series—that was encouraging—but Lolich ended the game by striking out Maris, pinch-hitting in the pitcher's spot, and getting Brock on a ground ball back to the mound. He was working his way out of McLain's shadow.

McLain, however, was not quite as finished as he had let on. He'd received another injection of cortisone after Game 4, in which he pitched only two-plus innings, and three days later here he was again, starting Game 6 back in St Louis. His control was sharp, and his support was generous.

The Tigers were already leading 3–0 when our starter, Ray Washburn, left in the third inning with no outs and two runners on. Larry Jaster, a young lefty who made his living by beating the Dodgers, replaced Washburn, and three batters later, after a grand slam by Northrup—the Slammer—it was 8–0. We couldn't ruin McLain's shutout until the ninth, by which time Kaline had also homered and Detroit had scored 13.

GAME 7, THE measure of the season, was on a Thursday. I was back with three days of rest, Lolich with two.

Lolich had thrown just 220 innings prior to the Series, and in that respect might have been a little fresher than I was, aside from the short turnaround. On the other hand, he wasn't accustomed to the strains of a compressed workload or the seventh game of a World Series. This was my third of those, and the other two had gone swimmingly. In fact, McCarver attributes our failures in Games 5 and 6 to the unhealthy sense of security that came with having me ready for Game 7. I felt pretty good about it myself, but 1968 had taught me never to count my runs before they've crossed the plate.

Game 7—appropriately, I suppose—was a '68 affair from the start. Flood stole a base in the bottom of the first and Cepeda reached on a walk, but we came up empty. When I fanned Northrup to end the top of the second, it broke Koufax's record of 29 strikeouts in a Series. McCarver walked to start the bottom of the inning, but Maris rolled into a double play, the first of seven straight Cardinals to ground out. The Tigers' first hit, by Stanley in the fourth, never left the infield.

All the while, there was a feeling that we were sure to get to Lolich in good time. He had led the American League in shutouts the year before—while he served with the Michigan National Guard, helping to protect a supply depot one night after a doubleheader, with Detroit burning around him—and he was a tough customer who typically struck out batters at about the same clip that I did; but this was his third start in eight days, without relief. He was shutting us down with a potbelly, a quick slider, and a sinking fastball that we consistently chased. And he wasn't even a natural left-hander.

The story goes that, when he was young enough to be riding a tricycle, he somehow crashed it into a motorcycle, which fell on him, breaking his collarbone. The accident put his right arm in a sling and the ball in his left, with which he eventually led his Babe Ruth youth team—he was from Portland, Oregon—to the national championship. Mickey must have been grateful to the motorcycle. By '68, he owned five Kawasakis.

As a lefty, Lolich came to idolize Whitey Ford, who happened to be the only pitcher with more World Series wins than I had. Mickey was ambitious; but even so, he was ready to quit the game before he reached the major leagues, the effect of having been hit in the face with a line drive. The Tigers persuaded him to stick it out by sending him back home to Portland to pitch for the team he used to serve as a batboy. While he was there, he was taught by Gerry Staley, a veteran right-hander, to use his sinker and keep the ball down and away.

In Game 7, he was doing that in spades. We did string a couple hits together in the sixth, however. Brock, leading off the inning, went the other way with one of those outside sinkers and singled to left field. At that point, Freehan walked out to the mound to talk. He said later that he asked Lolich if he could do anything for him, and Mickey said, yeah, you can get me a couple hamburgers between innings. I suspect they might also have discussed Brock's timing when he took off to steal second base, because when he did, Lolich threw to first and picked him off. After Javier lined out, Flood singled, and Lolich picked *him* off, too.

The game was still scoreless at that point, and when Kaline grounded to Shannon for the second out of the seventh inning, I had retired twenty of the twenty-one batters I'd faced. The twenty-second was Cash. He singled to right on a 3-2 fastball. Horton then singled to left on a first-pitch fastball, finding the hole between Shannon and Maxvill.

Tim had something to say about the situation. I listened and nodded. And threw an opening fastball to Northrup, whose home run in Game 4 was the only hit he'd produced against me in the Series.

This time, he sent a long fly to center field, to Flood's right and a little behind him. Curt may have had some momentary difficulty picking it out of the mass of white shirts around the ballpark. He began to step forward before lighting out laterally. On his path to the ball—he may have been trying to change his course, he may have hit a wet patch of grass, he may have gotten his feet tangled, I'm just not sure—he stumbled and nearly fell. A similar thing had happened to Northrup on a fly hit by Javier in the first inning, when we put two runners on base, but he'd been able to recover and make the play. Flood wasn't, mainly because Northrup had driven the ball too hard and far to allow it.

Cash and Horton scored, and after Curt's chase ended at the wall, Northrup rolled into third with a triple. Freehan followed by lifting a 2-2 breaking pitch to the left of Brock, who raced that way and reached in vain to his shoetops. When we regrouped in the dugout, we were down 3–0. Curt came over and tried to apologize, but I wouldn't let him. Not *him*. The way I saw it, if Curt Flood couldn't make a catch, it couldn't be made.

In the seventh, Northrup was charged with an error when he couldn't handle a ball Shannon hit his way; but Lolich was unfazed. We kept thinking that, pretty soon, as tired as he had to be, he was bound to bring the ball up in the zone. It never came up. Maybe it was *because* he was so tired. A sinkerballer, like a curveballer, gets in trouble when he's too strong and puts so much velocity on the pitch that it doesn't have a chance to do its thing. Lolich had no concerns along those lines.

He was still working the corners and the knees in the eighth when, in what I considered to be a thoughtful gesture—although it might have just been a baseball move, because I swung the bat pretty decently against lefties—Red allowed me to hit. Or strike out, as it happened. We went down quietly once again.

I appreciated the opportunity to finish the game, but I was spent. Horton shot a one-out single into left, Northrup rolled one up the middle, and Don Wert drove in the Tigers' fourth run with a line drive to center. That brought Lolich to the plate with two outs, and the St. Louis fans applauded him. As much as it hurt, I had to grudgingly second the emotion. A right-handed batter, he popped out to Javier. When I walked off the field for the last time in 1968, there were no handshakes or back slaps.

Lolich was an out away from a remarkable shutout when Shannon homered to left. He had to settle for a remarkable 4–1 victory, and the Series MVP award. *My* MVP award. It was the first time I'd left a World Series without it.

Truthfully, *that's* the game I recall most vividly from the Year of the Pitcher. All the others were followed by another. Baseball is that way: The games keep coming. You train and plan and grunt and ache and win or lose and do it again five days later, if you're the guy who gets the ball; three or four, maybe, if it's a World Series. It's unrelenting. It's hard.

What's harder, though, is when it's October, and a game goes wrong, and you don't *get* to do it again. You have to live with that one.

It's unrelenting.

Bibliography

Allen, Kevin. *The People's Champion: Willie Horton*. Wayne, Mich.: Immortal Investments, 2004.

Angell, Roger. *Late Innings*. New York: Simon & Schuster, 1982.

Armour, Mark. "Denny McLain." SABR Baseball Biography Project.

Associated Press. "Gibson Gets His Car, Says Brock Real Hero." *Daytona Beach Morning Journal*, October 17, 1967.

Baker, Russell. "Conventional View Is Taken of Game." *New York Times*, October 3, 1968.

Barra, Allen. "How Curt Flood Changed Baseball and Killed His Career in the Process." *The Atlantic*, July 12, 2011.

Baseball-reference.com.

Bishop, Bill. "Pat Dobson." SABR Baseball Biography Project.

Blau, Cliff. "The Real First-Year Player Draft." *Summer 2010 Baseball Research Journal*, 2010.

Brock, Lou, and Franz Schulze. *Stealing Is My Game*. Englewood Cliffs, N.J.: Prentice Hall, 1976.

Butler, Hal. *The Willie Horton Story*. New York: Julian Messner, 1970.

Calcaterra, Craig. "Rearguing the Curt Flood Case." nbcsports.com, May 24, 2013.

Bibliography

Cantor, George. *The Tigers of '68*. Dallas: Taylor Publishing, 1997.

Cepeda, Orlando, with Charles Einstein. *My Ups and Downs in Baseball*. New York: G. P. Putnam's Sons, 1968.

Cizik, John. "Dick McAuliffe." SABR Baseball Biography Project.

Donovan, Loretta. "Dal Maxvill." SABR Baseball Biography Project.

Durso, Joseph. "Cool Pitcher and Victor over Pain." *New York Times*, October 3, 1968.

Feldmann, Doug. *El Birdos*. Jefferson, N.C.: McFarland, 2007.

Fenech, Anthony. "Mickey Stanley to Receive First Tigers Legends Award." *Detroit Free Press*, January 9, 2015.

Fleitz, David. "Eddie Mathews." SABR Baseball Biography Project.

Flood, Curt, with Richard Carter. *The Way It Is*. New York: Pocket Books, 1972.

Freehan, Bill. *Behind the Mask*. New York: Popular Library, 1970.

Frost, Mark. *Game Six*. New York: Hyperion, 2009.

Gagnon, Dave. "Gates Brown." SABR Baseball Biography Project.

Geisler, Paul, Jr. "Julian Javier." SABR Baseball Biography Project.

Gibson, Bob, with Phil Pepe. *From Ghetto to Glory*. Englewood Cliffs, N.J.: Prentice Hall, 1968.

Gibson, Bob, with Lonnie Wheeler. *Stranger to the Game: The Autobiography of Bob Gibson*. New York: Viking, 1994.

Gibson, Bob, and Reggie Jackson, with Lonnie Wheeler. *Sixty Feet, Six Inches: A Hall of Fame Pitcher and a Hall of Fame Hitter Talk About How the Game Is Played*. New York: Doubleday, 2009.

Golenbock, Peter. *The Spirit of St. Louis*. New York: Avon, 2000.

Gregory, Robert. *Diz*. New York: Viking, 1992.

Halberstam, David. *October 1964*. New York: Fawcett, 1994.

Hawkins, Jim. *Al Kaline*. Chicago: Triumph Books, 2010.

Holmes, Dan. "Willie Horton." SABR Baseball Biography Project.

Kates, Maxwell. "Norm Cash." SABR Baseball Biography Project.

Kaufman, Michael T. *1968*. New York: Roaring Brook Press, 2009.

Keri, Jonah. "Forty Years Later, Gibson's 1.12 ERA Remains Magic Number." espn.com, February 7, 2008.

Kurlansky, Mark. *1968: The Year That Rocked the World*. New York: Random House, 2004.

Lassman, Mike. "Tommy Matchick." SABR Baseball Biography Project.

Leggett, William. "Detroit Is Having That Dream Again." *Sports Illustrated*, July 1, 1968.

———. "The Tigers See Too Much Red." *Sports Illustrated*, October 14, 1968.

———. "Those Big Tiger Muscles." *Sports Illustrated*, June 5, 1967.

Lieb, Frederick. *The St. Louis Cardinals*. New York: G. P. Putnam's Sons, 1944.

Markusen, Bruce. "Norm Cash's '72 Topps Baseball Card Captured Everything I Loved About Him." detroitathletic.com, June 4, 2014.

———. *The Orlando Cepeda Story*. Houston: Piñata Books, 2001.

McCann, Kevin. "Mike Shannon." SABR Baseball Biography Project.

McCarver, Tim, with Jim Moskovitz and Danny Peary. *Tim McCarver's Diamond Gems.* New York: McGraw-Hill, 2008.

McCarver, Tim, with Danny Peary. *Tim McCarver's Baseball for Brain Surgeons and Other Fans.* New York: Villard, 1998.

McCarver, Tim, with Ray Robinson. *Oh, Baby, I Love It!* New York: Villard, 1987.

McLain, Denny, with Dave Diles. *Nobody's Perfect.* New York: Dial, 1975.

Milner, John. "Don Wert." SABR Baseball Biography Project.

Morris, Bill. *Motor City Burning.* New York: Pegasus Books, 2014.

Nechal, Jerry. "Mickey Stanley." SABR Baseball Biography Project.

Nowlin, Bill, and John Harry Stahl, eds., Society for American Baseball Research. *Drama and Pride in the Gateway City.* Lincoln: University of Nebraska Press, 2013.

Ogden, David, and Joel Nathan Rosen, eds. *Reconstructing Fame.* Jackson: University Press of Mississippi, 2008.

Okrent, Daniel. *Nine Innings.* New York: McGraw-Hill, 1985.

Olsen, Jack. "The Torments of Excellence." *Sports Illustrated,* May 11, 1964.

Pruden, Bill. "Roger Maris." SABR Baseball Biography Project.

Ruppert, Jim. "Summer of 1968 Still a Dream for Denny McLain." *State Journal-Register* (Springfield, Ill.), June 21, 2014.

Sargent, Jim. "Jim Northrup." SABR Baseball Biography Project.

Sloope, Terry. "Curt Flood." SABR Baseball Biography Project.

Smith, Curt. *America's Dizzy Dean.* St. Louis: Bethany Press, 1978.

Stewart, Mark. "Orlando Cepeda." SABR Baseball Biography Project.

Strecker, Trey. "Bill Freehan." SABR Baseball Biography Project.

"Tiger Untamed." *Time,* September 13, 1968.

Tomasik, Mark. "How Tim McCarver Became a Cardinal at 17." *Retro-Simba,* December 10, 2013.

Vecsey, George. "Gibson Unaware of Breaking Record Until Message Flashes on Scoreboard." *New York Times,* October 3, 1968.

Verducci, Tom. "The Left Arm of God." *Sports Illustrated,* July 12, 1999.

Vorperian, John. "Don McMahon." SABR Baseball Biography Project.

Waddell, Nick. "Al Kaline." SABR Baseball Biography Project.

"The Washington Scene." *Jet,* August 7, 1969.

Wendel, Tim. *Summer of '68.* Boston: Da Capo, 2012.

Williams, Dave. "Tim McCarver." SABR Baseball Biography Project.

796.357
GIB

STONEHAM

NOV 2 1 2015

PUBLIC LIBRARY